GET
UP
and
GO!

GET UP
and
GO!

Devotionals for Mission

TOM SIKES

iUniverse®

GET UP AND GO!
DEVOTIONALS FOR MISSION

iUniverse books may be ordered through booksellers or by contacting:

iUniverse
1663 Liberty Drive
Bloomington, IN 47403
www.iuniverse.com
1-800-Authors (1-800-288-4677)

ISBN: 978-1-4917-6646-0 (sc)
ISBN: 978-1-4917-6645-3 (e)

Library of Congress Control Number: 2015907355

Print information available on the last page.

iUniverse rev. date: 5/30/2015

*To Sammy Clark, who invited me
into ministry and mission*

CONTENTS

Get Up and Go with the Apostles

PREFACE

"Get up and go!" God said those words often to people in the Bible. He says the same words today. God calls us inward through devotional reading; he then sends us outward in the Spirit to join him in ministry. This devotional book blends meditation with mission.

Come inside, and meet people that God called to get up and go into the world with hope and inspiration. See how their stories shape us for our mission today.

I encourage you to think along the lines of mission as you read scripture. These devotionals are intended merely to plant seeds. They are brief and thought provoking with some twists along the way. At the end of the book, I offer suggested resources to help if you would like to learn more about the missional church and opportunities for mission trips or projects.

EVERYBODY IS A MISSIONARY

I have been in pastoral ministry for more than thirty years and have received my doctorate in missions. I have enjoyed helping people discover their mission fields of home, school, work, and beyond. I follow the missional church model that offers these points:

1. Everybody has a calling. How can people discover their missional vocations?

2. A missional church is more interested in the sending capacity of its members than the seating capacity of the sanctuary.

3. We are called to *be* the Gospel, *do* the Gospel, and, lastly, *say* the Gospel.

4. Here is a benediction we use as a missional church that emphasizes the sending of members as missionaries:

> You go nowhere by accident.
> Wherever you go, God is sending you.
> God has a purpose in your being there.
> And he has given his Holy Spirit to you!

Each devotional is from either the Gospels or the book of Acts, using the New International Version of the Bible unless otherwise noted. I offer some highlights, questions, and a prayer. At the end of this book are some resources that go deeper into the missions.

Let's get up and go!

INTRODUCTION

Are you looking for a deeper purpose in life? Beyond getting a paycheck and having a roof over your head and food in your system, are you being fulfilled? Maybe you are stuck in the middle of nowhere.

NOWHERE IS NOW HERE!

You are now here. Come inside. Discover how God called people who were in a rut and how they jumped at the chance to join God in mission around them. From Nicodemus to the woman at the well and others from many more story lines, they all were invited to go beyond where they were.

Jesus says, "Come follow me." Let's get up and go!

GET
UP

and

GO

with Jesus

MISSION POSSIBLE

> Jesus called his twelve disciples to him
> and gave them authority to drive out
> evil spirits and to heal every disease and
> sickness.
> —Matthew 10:1

Have you ever described yourself as a missionary? God does. God takes normal people and turns them into missionaries at home, at work, or at school and beyond.

Let's set some framework for this book of devotionals. We will rephrase these themes, as God would shape these principles differently with each person he calls. Here we discover the threefold commission of disciples as they discern their purposes:

1. Jesus *called* the twelve to himself. Twelve is the number for completeness. It is the number of the tribes of Jacob. It had meaning, and the disciples were familiar with that number. He called them to himself to see God as a person, to experience

his grace, to dance at weddings, and to laugh and learn.

2. Jesus *shaped* them by giving them authority in his name. He molded them for mission by giving them power—not in their own name but in his name.

3. Jesus *sent* them to heal. This concept is crucial. It was not a club to gather but a church to scatter. Two by two he sent them, with purpose and peace.

To be a Christian is to be called, shaped, and sent.

- How does God call us these days?
- What are ways that God molds us?
- Where do you want God to send you today?
- Where do you *not* want God to send you?
- Which of these questions is the toughest to answer?

PRAYER

Every day is a new day for mission! Help me to sense my calling, to be chiseled and groomed to be more like Christ, and send me to meet people who need encouragement and hope—I pray.

GET UP, TAKE YOUR MAT, AND GO HOME

Jesus stepped into a boat, crossed over and came to his own town. Some men brought to him a paralytic, lying on a mat. When Jesus saw their faith, he said to the paralytic, "Take heart, son; your sins are forgiven." At this, some of the teachers of the law said to themselves, "This fellow is blaspheming!" Knowing their thoughts, Jesus said, "Why do you entertain evil thoughts in your hearts? Which is easier: to say, 'Your sins are forgiven,' or to say, 'Get up and walk'? But so that you may know that the Son of Man has authority on earth to forgive sins …" Then he said to the paralytic, "Get up, take your mat and go home." And the man got up and went home. When the crowd saw this, they were filled with awe; and they praised God.
—Matthew 9:1–8

The one who would climb a cross would crisscross the waters. He looked beyond the whitecaps toward the shores for people who needed him. Are you waving to him now to come to you? If he did come, what would he do for you? Let's see how he treated this man who was paralyzed. What is it that keeps us down and out?

Jesus offered a threefold call to this paralyzed man. Imagine him speaking like this:

1. *Get up.* In other words, I see that you are down. I am aware of the disease that keeps you down physically and emotionally. I say to you words that are opposite of what you or others say. I am able to heal you, but you must do your part. Get up.

2. *Take your mat.* Don't leave it down there, or you might want to fall back on it. I am aware of your human tendency to fall back into old routines. Take the old life with you, and perhaps throw it in the garbage.

3. *Go home.* The first people who need to see you whole are your family members. Watch their faces as you walk in the kitchen door. Your mission field begins at home before anywhere else. Your sins are all forgiven, so don't live in shame anymore. Smile big, dance in the kitchen, and feel the freedom of my love. Let them love you and hold you and support you. Thank them for their care while you

were paralyzed. Prepare the fatted calf! It is time to celebrate!

He had the best of both worlds. He met God, and God did not ignore him or chastise him. God loved him and gave him a new lease on life. Today, God says the same to us. He loves for us to get up, take our mats, and go home.

Would you like to be set free too? "Take heart. Your sins are forgiven." Which sins come to mind? To continue our mission, God forgives our sins of commission and omission!

The good news is after we confess our sins and turn from our wrong ways, God remembers those sins no more. They are gone like the paralysis.

PRAYER

I want to get up, take my mat, and go home. I want to be set free in your forgiveness, Lord. I offer you my sins, and in return you give me grace. It is costly grace, for it cost you your life on the cross. I am ready to move again, to get up and be alive!

MEET THE MESSENGER

The beginning of the gospel about Jesus Christ, the Son of God: It is written in Isaiah the prophet: "I will send my messenger ahead of you, who will prepare your way, a voice of one calling in the desert, 'Prepare the way for the Lord, make straight paths for him.'" And so John came, baptizing in the desert region and preaching a baptism of repentance for the forgiveness of sins. The whole Judean countryside and all the people of Jerusalem went out to him. Confessing their sins, they were baptized by him in the Jordan River. John wore clothing made of camel's hair, with a leather belt around his waist, and he ate locusts and wild honey. And this was his message: "After me will come one more powerful than I, the thongs of whose sandals I am not worthy to stoop down and untie. I baptize you with

water, but he will baptize you with the
Holy Spirit."
—Mark 1:1–8

Before God sent Jesus, he sent his cousin John. Malachi
3:1 reads, "See, I will send my messenger who will prepare
the way before me." The reason it is the last book of the
Old Testament is because it would escort us into the New
Testament and the story of the Messiah. And sure enough,
the story of Jesus's ministry began with the messenger
who prepared the way.

- Why did the Messiah need a messenger to go in
  front to prepare the way?
- Who would have thought it would be his cousin?

The Gospel began in a desert with a wildflower. In bleak
barrenness appeared someone truly alive! Nothing could
live in such surroundings for very long. But John thrived
in the dryness, identifying with their spiritual thirst for
a God who was ready to wash them of their greed and
corruption, jealousies, and more. John was a refreshing
voice in a strange setting. They would come from near and
far to run to the waters and immerse themselves in the
river of newness. They would … *get up and go.*

While on a mission trip to the lower ninth ward of New
Orleans with Rev. Vance Moore following Hurricane
Katrina, we met seventy-eight-year-old Pastor Howard
Washington sitting on a five-gallon bucket putting copper
back in a room after it had been stolen. He built that

church when he was in his thirties. Then he had to build it again. The water inside his church reached the ceiling, and most of the Sheetrock and walls were ruined. But there was one wall that survived. It was the baptistery, of all places. And on that wall was the image of cousins John and Jesus in the River Jordan. Guess who painted that image decades before? It was the cousin of Pastor Washington. When we arrived, a member of our church, Eleanor Hinson, heard the whisper by God to get up and go buy paint and touch up that painting. With teenagers beside her, they repaired that image. It was restored out of the water for another generation. Take a mission trip to see it for yourself at the Greater New Jerusalem Missionary Baptist Church on Alabo Street. You just might see Jesus.

Where will you see Jesus today? Where have you seen God at work around you?

PRAYER

From the birth waters of Creation to the stormy waters of disaster, you continue to create. Thank you for the call to join you in your mission. I pause to give thanks for the following people who show me the love of God and are called into mission.

FROM WATER
TO THE WILD

At that time Jesus came from Nazareth in Galilee and was baptized by John in the Jordan. As Jesus was coming up out of the water, he saw heaven being torn open and the Spirit descending on him like a dove. And a voice came from heaven: "You are my Son, whom I love; with you I am well pleased." At once, the Spirit sent him out into the desert, and he was in the desert forty days, being tempted by Satan. He was with the wild animals, and angels attended him.
—Mark 1:9–12

As Jesus was coming up out of the water, the skies opened, and a voice trumpeted words of identity, origin, purpose, and destiny. "You are mine!" But before Jesus could jump for joy, before he could get puffed up with pride, what happened? The Spirit immediately told Jesus to "get up and go" into the desert. The word is *propelled*. He was launched into the wild, the desert, the craggy, dark wasteland to be tempted. Jesus was sent into the open to be vulnerable to the deceiver. One minute Jesus was immersed in all the water he could want. The next minute his lips were cracking and his throat was parched. He was suffering for water in the desert.

The Enemy had his sights set on Jesus as he trudged through the desert. High aloft a cliff, he had a clear shot to kill the Savior and his mission to save the world. From the lush Garden of Eden to the jagged cliffs, the Enemy coiled, ready to strike. Jesus was aware. He relied on his lessons in Hebrew school and recited from the scrolls of his youth. He remained true thanks to his humility, his respect for his Father, and his deep sense of his mission. Jesus would prevail.

- What do you bring with you in your times of temptation?
- Do you give in without a fight?
- Do you challenge your inner thoughts and seek to have self-control?
- How long can you hold out before giving in?

You have a God who can relate to your journey into your wilderness. He loves you and is here to encourage you to be strong in the face of adversity. Do you have a scripture you can recite when you are tempted? It has been the weapon of choice by Jesus and Christians ever since. Consider this one: "I can do all things through Jesus Christ who gives me strength!" (Philippians 4:13).

PRAYER

As you send me from exhilarating moments of my life, you also send me to challenging moments too. Life is not easy as your follower. I know that full well. You have a way of shaping me, sometimes surrounding me with your grace and sometimes leaving me (it seems) out in the open to see where I place my trust. Where am I now, Lord? If I go to the highest heavens, you are there. If I sink to the abyss with the snakes, you are there.

COME, FOLLOW ME!

As Jesus walked beside the Sea of Galilee, he saw Simon and his brother Andrew casting a net into the lake, for they were fishermen. "Come, follow me," Jesus said, "and I will make you fishers of men [people]." At once they left their nets and followed him.
—Mark 1:16–18

Lace up your shoes a bit tighter. The Gospel of Mark is a very brisk walk with Jesus, and there is no time to lose. Jesus was on the move, and rarely do we read that Jesus stayed for long periods of time in one place. He left his Nazareth shop to follow his call into mission. Finally away from the manufacturing business, Jesus was seen walking the shores of a lake north of Jerusalem breathing the fresh air and perhaps skipping flat rocks across the surface. One day soon, he would walk on that surface.

Jesus settled around this lake and began to seek out disciples who would follow his every move. As with other rabbis, students would sit at the feet of their teacher and glean knowledge and pick the fruits of his wisdom. Perhaps Jesus was wearing a prayer shawl as he looked out on the waters seeing a set of brothers casting a net into the sea. Were they arguing like brothers often do? Or were they silently mending their nets, questioning if they would ever get to leave that fishing village?

They were totally unaware that God was watching them at work. Simon and Andrew had it down pat; their chemistry enabled them not to have to talk as they threw the nets. They were in a rhythm, but underneath they were searching for a greater meaning.

God knew that too. Jesus cuffed his hands to his mouth, and his voice carried over the still waters. "Come, follow me."

In other words, get up from your boat, and come in my direction. A word of invitation began with God, and when God invites, who can turn down God? Simon and Andrew looked at each other, and before they knew it, they were walking in the footsteps of God.

- Is God watching you at work?
- What does he see?
- What does he hear?

PRAYER

What would happen, God, if you came to my workplace and called me to leave it? Would I do that? I have too many things on my plate, too many irons in the fire. Plus, how would I get paid? Did Simon and Andrew think about that too? I wish they had asked more questions about what was involved before leaving their business. But maybe they knew inside that God was going to take care of them. And he did … and he will with me too. Right, God? Maybe I can learn from these brothers, that when you call me to follow …

MATTHEW'S CALL

> As Jesus went on from there, he saw a
> man named Matthew sitting at the tax
> collector's booth. "Follow me," he told him,
> and Matthew got up and followed him.
> —Matthew 9:9

We were leaving lunch one day, casually walking down the sidewalk and window-shopping, when we spotted Jesus looking into the window of a business. It was the office of Matt, the much-hated man who took our taxes and then some. Matt made our stomachs turn. He knew it too. We could see the guilt on his face when we saw him at the café.

Why would Jesus want to see Matthew other than to take him behind the woodshed and condemn him?

Jesus had just healed that paralytic and told him that his sins were forgiven, and the man was no longer as he had been. He was no longer plastered to a bed but was alive and able to move and dance and engage back into the community. We had no idea we would see that theme of grace played out again in the life of Matthew.

Jesus knocked on the door. No one came; there was just a gravelly voice that shouted, "Go away! I'm busy!" Jesus knocked again, and this time Matthew grumbled, getting up from his chair to see who was bothering him. Jesus went into that office. We watched and waited for the fireworks. The purest man alive would meet the corrupt and greedy man sitting at the booth. Five minutes later, we saw it.

Matthew was coming out of his office without his trusty briefcase. He rattled his keys and locked the door behind him. Arm in arm, Jesus and Matthew went walking down the street. We heard later that Matthew never came back. He followed Jesus that day as a disciple. When he locked his past of greed, he opened himself to grace. Of all people, Matthew would be called by Jesus to become an apostle: called to be sent, to proclaim hope, and perform miracles ... and write the first Gospel!

If God could use Matthew, then God can use ___. Fill in the blank. It might be your name, or it might even be someone you despise. Think on that one today.

PRAYER

Lord, if you were to come to my office asking me to get up and follow you, how would it change me? Would I let you walk out alone? Would I stay behind my comfortable desk?

Lord, have you walked into my boardroom or my business and called me to use my skills to do your work? If you could use Matthew, can you use me today? What about my enemy?

BAR STOOL MINISTRY

> While Jesus was having dinner at Matthew's house, many tax collectors and "sinners" came and ate with him and his disciples. When the Pharisees saw this, they asked his disciples, "Why does your teacher eat with tax collectors and 'sinners'?" On hearing this, Jesus said, "It is not the healthy who need a doctor, but the sick. But go and learn what this means: 'I desire mercy, not sacrifice.' 'For I have not come to call the righteous, but sinners.'"
>
> —Matthew 9:10–13

"Hey, Bart and Esther!" Matt shouted as he ran up to them on Main Street. "I'm throwing a party tonight at seven and wanted you to come to my house. I'm bringing a new friend of mine. His name is Jeshua bar Joseph (Jesus son of Joseph). Come and meet him, okay?" He then invited us too. Matthew would go into the juke joints and the bathhouses, inviting his friends to share his joy.

People sensed something had happened to their friend. They were curious.

When Jesus was called out of the carpenter's shop, he was called not only to the synagogue. Sure, he taught there and healed there, but that was not going to confine God's message. Buildings do not box in God's power and mercy and grace. The walls between the church and the street are porous. The winds of God sweep from steeple to people. And those people include the worst of the worst.

Jesus was willing to go to the homes of the tax collectors and sinners. He was willing to sit at a bar stool and be himself in Matthew's home. Matthew had thrown a party for his friends and wanted everyone to meet this Jesus—a real man with a real faith and sincerity like no one he had ever met. And Jesus brought his other disciples too.

We often struggle to remember this call: to *get up and go* be with the sinners.

We are called to share the hope of God outside the sanctuary and the stained-glass windows if we want to be a church. Members are called as missionaries. They gather in the Spirit in order to be scattered by the Spirit into the dark rooms with the light of good news. They are sent into the culture to share the Christ, just like Jesus did.

God came not to the righteous but to the ones who were missing the mark. You and I know that. We were there at Matthew's party. Why? Jesus was friends with sinners.

And God came toward us that night and still does today. What an honor it was to be included and to see Matthew come alive through Jesus Christ. We came alive too!

PRAYER

Jesus, call me beyond into the dark places, not to judge but to invite others into mission.

THREE IN ONE

A ruler came and knelt before Jesus and said, "My daughter has just died. But come and put your hand on her, and she will live." Jesus got up and went with him, and so did his disciples. Just then a woman who had been subject to bleeding for twelve years came up behind him and touched the edge of his cloak. She said to herself, "If I only touch his cloak, I will be healed." Jesus turned and saw her. "Take heart, daughter," he said, "your faith has healed you." And the woman was healed from that moment. When Jesus entered the ruler's house and saw the flute players and the noisy crowd, he said, "Go away. The girl is not dead but asleep." But they laughed at him. After the crowd had been put outside, he went in and took the girl by the hand. She got up. News of this spread through all that region.
—Matthew 9:18–26

We have three stories of mission in one.

Story 1: A father sensed God's call to *get up and* go find Jesus, who might be able to raise his daughter from the dead. He showed remarkable faith and boldness. While the others were preparing her funeral, he went in search of Christ.

Story 2: A woman sensed God's call to *get up and go* toward Jesus and believe that if she just touched the thread of his prayer shawl tassel, she could be well. Jesus had so much power around him that even touching a string could heal her of her bleeding disorder.

Story 3: The flute players were told by Jesus to *get up and go* away. Whoa. His command was far different than the other two. These people laughed in the face of God. He sent them, all right. He sent them away from him. We don't see that happening often.

Where are you in this story? Would you rush to find Jesus in the moment of death? Would you reach out and touch the hem of the holy garment to find relief? You probably have done both in your lifetime. These stories are our stories.

What about the flute players? Have you ever questioned if God could raise the dead to life? Do you believe he cannot do it today? Flute players are all around us. Sometimes we need to move them out of our lives so we can put our hope in Jesus.

Can God bring the dead to life? Are all things possible with God?

PRAYER

God, where am I in this story? Am I a parent who prays to you to restore my child, who is suffering with addiction or dying on the inside from a difficult past? Am I the one who has dealt with losing my life source, slowly bleeding to death with disease, or dis-ease? Perhaps I am the flute player attracted to other people's crises, or am I with the ones laughing at the idea that God heals today? Again, where am I in this story, Lord?

SENSELESS

As Jesus went on from there, two blind men followed him, calling out, "Have mercy on us, Son of David!" When he had gone indoors, the blind men came to him, and he asked them, "Do you believe that I am able to do this?" "Yes, Lord," they replied. Then he touched their eyes and said, "According to your faith will it be done to you" and their sight was restored. Jesus warned them sternly, "See that no one knows about this." But they went out and spread the news about him all over the region. While they were going out, a man who was demon-possessed and could not talk was brought to Jesus. And when the demon was driven out, the man who had been mute spoke. The crowd was amazed and said, "Nothing like this has ever been seen in Israel."

—Matthew 9:27–33

If you had to lose one of your senses, would you rather be blind or mute? God came toward those with disabilities. He was especially sent to people when they were unable or disabled. Two blind men and a mute would meet that day. Their paths would converge along the pathway of Christ.

First, the blind men were together. Where did they meet? How did they get blind? It was the blind leading the blind. Loss does that. We are united when we are without. Divorce recovery workshops can bring new friends into our lives. Hospital stays can offer a chance to enter a new world of injury, disease, and recovery with others in the same condition. Addictive personalities gather in a room daily in an AA meeting and discover they are not alone. Friendships emerge.

They were drawn to Jesus. They could not see him yet still followed. I imagine the swimming pool game of Marco Polo. You close your eyes and shout "Marco." The one who is "it" has to shout out "Polo" and try to not let the other touch him. It is a game of blind tag. Such was the case in this story. They yelled every city block, "Jesus," and he said, "Here I am." And because of their deep faith, he touched each of their eyes. They tagged Jesus. He let them tag him so he could heal the thing in their life that was mission—vision.

None of us has seen the physical Jesus either. And yet we continue to call his name. He stops and allows us to touch him so he can touch the things in our lives that are lacking. What is it in your life that you need restored?

As they were skipping home, immediately Jesus was cornered by other people asking him to do another miracle. He had no time to rest, to recover, to renew. Jesus was face-to-face with evil. Possessed by darkness, a man consumed by hatred was brought to him.

- Did Jesus bristle?
- Did he have a flashback to his experience of facing evil in the desert after his baptism?

"The demon was driven out." This statement signified extreme effort, action, force, power, and persistence. People cared enough about this man to get up and go find Jesus and bring the mute to the Messiah.

- So which miracle touches you today—that of the blind men or the mute?
- Would you rather be blind or mute?
- What are some ways we are blind or mute right now?

PRAYER

God, please take my eyes that I may see people and their goodness. Take my mouth and help me to speak words of encouragement and hope—I pray.

THE SWOOSH

Now there was a man of the Pharisees
named Nicodemus, a member of the
Jewish ruling council. He came to Jesus at
night and said, "Rabbi, we know you are a
teacher who has come from God. For no
one could perform the miraculous signs
you are doing if God were not with him."
—John 3:1–2

Do you know that Nike is in the Bible?

The name Nicodemus came from two words in Greek:

1. *Nike* means *victory.*
2. *Demus* means *over the people.*

Nicodemus was a Pharisee, a separated scholar, a Torah-
keeper. He was obeying every law under Moses. While
Nicodemus was successful, he did not feel significant.
Something was missing in his life, and he knew it.

You and I were walking down the street that night looking at the moon, talking about the good meal of lamb gyros we had just eaten, when across the street we saw a man in a robe sneaking outside his house. He obviously did not want anyone to see him, but we did. We followed him out of curiosity. He clung to the walls going down Third Avenue. He made a left turn and found who he was looking for. It was Jesus, sitting on a rail in a backyard. He was all alone.

We heard him ask the question, "Rabbi, we know you are a teacher, but you perform miracles. God is with you. I am intrigued by you, Jesus." And there they had a long conversation that would change more lives than any other dialogue in scripture. We listened intently. Jesus summarized the reason he was on earth. It changed our lives that night. It has transformed people ever since. The most famous scripture in the Bible was recorded that night, thanks to the man named Nicodemus.

Since that night, aren't we still curious about Jesus? Do you also come to Jesus at night when no one is aware? What do you say to God as you stare at your ceiling trying to go to sleep? Or maybe your prayer time is when you walk or run at night.

The next time you lace up your Nike running shoes, think of Nicodemus. The question to ask when you see a swoosh symbol is, Am I running to Jesus or away from Jesus?

PRAYER

God, hear my prayers as I answer that question. Help me not to always have to be victorious over people. I come to you now like Nicodemus did, with heartfelt questions and the desire to be born anew.

THE COMPASS OF COMPASSION

Jesus went through all the towns and villages, teaching in their synagogues, preaching the good news of the kingdom and healing every disease and sickness. When he saw the crowds, he had compassion on them, because they were harassed and helpless, like sheep without a shepherd. Then he said to his disciples, "The harvest is plentiful but the workers are few. Ask the Lord of the harvest, therefore, to send out workers into the harvest field."

—Matthew 9:35–38

Jesus went. He was a *get up and go* kind of man, aware that his time on earth was short. Jesus did not sit around or spend all his time in meetings managing his ministry. He focused on people and was moved by the Spirit to help those who needed him. He taught in the faith communities, and he healed every disease and sickness ... not half of the sicknesses but *all* of them!

What did Jesus do as he went? His ministry could be summed up as teaching, preaching, and reaching. He revealed his threefold mission as he got up and went! He was a transient, a circuit rider, a traveling salesman giving away the Gospel for free. How did he keep track of his distances and his mileage? Did he ever stop and ask for directions?

He had a compass of compassion. That is what led him from one place to the next. It was not obligation but opportunity. He was commissioned through compassion. And he sought others to join him in his mission. "The harvest is plentiful, but where are the workers?"

- Are we the workers? Has God called us? Where is the harvest?
- Do you want to leap up and say that you will be a worker for his ministry?
- If so, where is God positioning you right now in your community?

PRAYER

Jesus, we tend to want you to do all the walking and talking. We are not good at speaking in public or staying compassionate with strangers. We don't pray in public very well, and we prefer to be behind the scenes. But you are looking for people out front, getting up and going, leading. Are you calling me to step it up? The harvest around me is plentiful, as people today are searching for purpose and meaning. Call me to step it up and step it out!

PACKING LIGHT

These twelve Jesus sent out with the following instructions: "Do not go among the Gentiles or enter any town of the Samaritans. Go rather to the lost sheep of Israel. As you go, preach the message: 'The kingdom of heaven is near.' Heal the sick, raise the dead, cleanse those who have leprosy, drive out demons. Freely you have received, freely give. Do not take along any gold or silver or copper in your belts; take no bag for the journey, or extra tunic, or sandals or a staff; for the worker is worth his keep."
—Matthew 10:5–10

Jesus called the two of us at Matthew's party. He invited us to join him in the mission field. We would be traveling a lot, so we went to buy our gear—shoes, backpack, a water bottle. We needed good socks and a sleeping bag, and what about our medicines? We were fired up to go on the mission trip with Christ. Jesus would send us together. We leaned in to hear where that would be. Would it be Central America or Africa? Jesus approached us and tapped us on the shoulders. "I send you ... to your neighborhood." What? We were ready to sail the seven seas, to scale tall mountains, and he was calling us to stay around home?

That was how Christianity began. Jesus sent out the new disciples around the corner to people just like themselves. They began their mission in areas that were familiar. The mission field here is just as important as the mission field there. It is on our streets, in our subdivision, around the corner. But as we go near, we carry with us incredible abilities to do great things for people—to remind folks that God is near, to heal the infirm, to be part of resurrection, to cleanse the ones ostracized by disease, to get mad at evil around us. We have received the spirit not of timidity but of power, and as we have received, we are to give back.

We got our call, looked at our backpacks, and decided to pack light. We didn't need much. Trust in God to provide. Don't load down on money or materials. We would have to rely on God, not on the goods. And Jesus grinned and said, "Be sent!"

PRAYER

Send me, Lord, today to make a difference, to engage in my world, to look around and see who is in my circle of influence. Who around me is sick or down or left outside in the cold? Who needs a smile, a word of encouragement, a Gospel experience of hope, joy, peace, and love? Send me, Lord, today. Remove the excess in my life. Simplify my life, I pray, so people may not see my logo but see the "Logos"—the word made flesh dwelling among us. Jesus in me.

SHAKE IT OFF

Whatever town or village you enter, search for some worthy person there and stay at his house until you leave. As you enter the home, give it your greeting. If the home is deserving, let your peace rest on it; if it is not, let your peace return to you. If anyone will not welcome you or listen to your words, shake the dust off your feet when you leave that home or town. I tell you the truth; it will be more bearable for Sodom and Gomorrah on the day of judgment than for that town. I am sending you out like sheep among wolves. Therefore be shrewd as snakes and innocent as doves.
—Matthew 10:11–16

Jesus was having a sales meeting, and around the table were gathered his new team of associates. The corporate office had invested in this team, a motley crew of fishermen, merchants, and accountants. Notice eight points of this passage:

1. They were given authority to speak on behalf of the president of the company.
2. They were to get up and go to places around them, to villages and cities by the shores of Galilee. Some homes would welcome them. Others would be skeptical.
3. They were to go door-to-door, place-to-place; they were on the move, faith in action.
4. They were sent to spread the word that God was near. They were missionaries sent.
5. But they were to be wise as serpents and innocent as doves. Jesus called them to be careful, to be alert and aware of their surroundings, and to not be naïve.
6. The twelve were to expect rejection. That was part of sales. "But if they reject you, they are rejecting the One who sent them, and woe to them," said Jesus.
7. The missionary's role is not to make people believe. The messenger simply heals, teaches, embraces, and shares the Gospel.
8. It is up to each recipient to accept or reject the Messiah. But if you are rejected, wipe your shoes, shake the dust off your feet, and carry on.

Would you apply for that job? What you sell is free. It seems too good to be true. Many people will reject your message. Shake it off and carry on!

PRAYER

As you send me, Lord, today, I seek to have the wisdom to know when to be wise and when to be innocent. Guard my day, and direct my path—I pray. Send me to people who need your light and love, and don't let me get disappointed when others don't feel they need you in their lives. Help me be calm and carry on with the Gospel message—and yes, to shake it off when I need to!

TO THE FAR SHORE

> Jesus crossed to the far shore of the Sea of Galilee [that is, the Sea of Tiberius], and a great crowd of people followed him because they saw the miraculous signs he had performed on the sick. Then Jesus went up on a mountainside and sat down with his disciples. The Jewish Passover Feast was near. When Jesus looked up and saw a great crowd coming toward him, he said to Philip, "Where shall we buy bread for these people to eat?" He asked this only to test him, for he already had in mind what he was going to do. Philip answered him, "Eight months' wages would not buy enough bread for each one to have a bite!"
> —John 6:1–7

From one side of the Sea of Galilee to the other, Jesus kept the boat from anchoring too long. It was time to go … to the far shore. God does that. Who is at the farthest shore but a great crowd? Today, God sees those far off, who are scampering up the hill to see God. They would be many, and they would be hungry. Notice what concerned Jesus. It was not his safety, his fear of being mobbed. His thoughts were on the people and who would feed them.

"Where shall we buy bread for these people to eat?" Philip would think of the baker and how much it would cost to buy that much bread. But Jesus was thinking of the Maker and the extreme love he would show to them by giving his only Son as the bread of life! Jesus had something in store, just not from the bread store! Philip was thinking logistically. God was thinking theologically. He already had in mind what he was going to do!

God goes to the farthest point to reach others. Maybe God is pulling up the anchor and going to the farthest point to reach you today. Are you on God's map? Can he find you? He will not only find you. He knows you hunger for answers, for peace, for purpose. Or maybe you are like Philip. You are close to Christ. It is time for you to feed someone else.

PRAYER

God, you are calling me today to go a little farther out ... to grow in my discipleship and join you in feeding those who are on the farthest shore. Or maybe I am the one in the crowd, starving spiritually and needing refreshment. Hear my prayer today of where I see myself in this passage ...

FEELING SMALL

Another of his disciples, Andrew, Simon
Peter's brother, spoke up, "Here is a boy
with five small barley loaves and two
small fish, but how far will they go among
so many?"
—John 6:8–9

Jesus had asked, "How are we to feed so many people?"
Philip had already pulled out his calculator to answer.
But here, we see another answer. It was by looking at the
resources already in their midst.

Andrew pulled a boy out of the masses because he saw he
had fish sandwiches.

- Did the boy's mother fix those fish and barley
  loaves and put them in his backpack for lunch?
- Did the little boy know that his lunch would
  become part of one of the greatest stories of all
  time?

Andrew was good at finding people. He had found his brother Simon, and introduced him to Christ. And here he found a kid with a backpack. Inside was not much. But it was food. He asked the question we ask too.

"Five small barley loaves and two small fishes for you, God, but how far will they go among so many?" Not only were there only a few, but they were small. A small boy, small loaves, and small fish are the recipe for large moments in the eyes of God!

We offer to God what we have. It does not look like much. But God can take a little and do a lot. Maybe today you are feeling a bit small inside. In a world that glamorizes the grandiose, you feel left out and unnoticed … just like this little boy with a few fish sandwiches.

Nothing is too small, and no one is too small. God would use the little to do the huge, thanks to Saint Andrew by the sea. Has Andrew found you and brought you to Jesus too?

PRAYER

I wonder what happened to that little boy who shared his lunch with Jesus. Did he go on and follow? Did he go home and explain what happened? Was he skipping school to see Jesus, who came his way? God, I thank you for this story of taking the small and doing great things with it. By bringing people into my life, I continually discover it's a small world after all.

ALL YOU CAN EAT

> Jesus said, "Have the people sit down."
> There was plenty of grass in that place,
> and they sat down, about five thousand
> of them. Jesus then took the loaves, gave
> thanks, and distributed to those who were
> seated as much as they wanted. He did the
> same with the fish.
> —John 6:10–11

You and I were in that crowd that day. We had no idea why we were told to sit down. But we did. We sat on the grass overlooking the Sea of Galilee. The gentle breeze blew our hair, and we looked out at the view. We took deep breaths, finally resting after the long walk to find Jesus. We were glad Jesus asked us to sit down.

We needed to rest. In our rush to find Christ, we forgot to pack food for the trip. And as we looked around, we saw no one else had food either. Out of the thousands of folks around us, everyone was empty-handed. We were told to be idle, to be still, and to do nothing. Just be. Like a sheep in the pasture of Psalm 23, Jesus had led us to the green pastures. Up the hill from the dusty roads below, we found ourselves with the Good Shepherd.

A child was brought to Jesus, who opened his lunch pail to share what he had. Jesus took the barley bread, blessed it, and broke it. And instead of eating it himself, what did we see him do? We got up on our knees for a better view. Jesus handed the loaves to the ones closest to him. There would be no way we would get fed. There were five thousand others around us. We felt ourselves getting flushed, anxious, and frustrated. Jesus was picking favorites? It wasn't fair. We were hundreds of feet from him. He wouldn't see us!

But in ten minutes the basket came toward us, and we looked inside. There was plenty of bread! Jesus leaned down to us and said, "Get all you can eat!" We reached in and doubled up with bread and fish! We looked over at the little boy whose meal had created a miracle. His head was bowed, and we heard him softly say these words: "God is great. God is good. And we thank him for our food. Amen."

Are you far from God right now? While others seem to be getting their fill with this Jesus, are you frustrated? Are you anxious that you are not getting fed? Come to him today, and know he loves you. He is coming your way right now. Reach out your hand—both hands—and get all you can eat of his grace. Receive him today into your heart.

PRAYER

Take this small moment, God, to feed me. It might be the biggest moment of my day or even of my life. I invite you into my life. Take my hunger and my frustrations. Replace them with your fulfilling grace. Hear my prayers now as I reach with both hands toward you.

LEFTOVERS

> When they had all had enough to eat, he said to his disciples, "Gather the pieces that are left over. Let nothing be wasted." So they gathered them and filled twelve baskets with the pieces of the five barley loaves left over by those who had eaten.
> —John 6:12–13

In the days of Moses, the nation of Israel ate manna bread that rained down from heaven. But they could eat only enough for a day. If it was stored, it would go stale. Here we see a parallel to that story as people gathered on a hillside and were fed with bread as it rained down from heaven into the lunch sack of a little boy. They all ate until they were filled. God does that for us. God wants us to "fill up"! Don't leave hungry.

And then ... stewardship happened. God said, "Get up and go and collect the remains. Take the leftovers and put them in baskets, not to throw away but to share with others."

Abundance in the present led to stewardship beyond. People loved that about Jesus. He was not concerned just about them and those who were around him. He was thinking about those who were not there and perhaps how he could share the leftovers.

Imagine that little boy taking bread and fish back home. His mom says, "Son, why didn't you eat the lunch I fixed you?"

And he said, "Mom, you won't believe what happened to me today! I shared my lunch with five thousand people plus! And Jesus asked me to bring some back to you because he wants to feed you too."

To this day, that meal has been feeding us with imagination and hope.

When we have leftovers from Communion each Sunday, what do we do with the wafers? In our tradition, the Communion meal is a memorial reminding us of Jesus taking the bread and cup and using it as symbols of his body and blood. We take the broken pieces and share them with the birds outside. I love to watch as the birds discover the bread. They somehow invite their friends to join them. It is one of the many highlights of my pastoral ministry when I look back on it. It is sharing the leftovers with the ones around us.

PRAYER

I want to fill up with your grain of grace and your fish of faith. It makes me look at food differently. What is on my plate that is left over? As I look at my cupboard and my closet, how can I share with those who are left out who could use my leftovers?

GOING WITHOUT GOD

When evening came, his disciples went down to the lake, where they got into a boat and set off across the lake for Capernaum. By now it was dark, and Jesus had not yet joined them. A strong wind was blowing and the waters grew rough. When they had rowed three or three and a half miles, they saw Jesus approaching the boat, walking on the water; and they were terrified. But he said, "It is I; don't be afraid." Then they were willing to take him into the boat, and immediately the boat reached the shore where they were heading.
—John 6:16–21

The day had been long. Jesus had fed five thousand with bread and bream. People wanted to make him "king," but he withdrew to a mountain. He was tired and needed to recharge his batteries. Even Jesus had to get away to be with his Father, away from people.

So there he was on the hillside taking deep breaths, talking in conversational form to his Dad. Maybe he was chuckling to himself, reliving the moment of feeding the five thousand. He grinned perhaps, thinking of Philip saying it was "eight months' wages to feed those folks." Andrew had offered a small solution. And Jesus had to laugh as he proved once again, "I can do all things …" (Philippians 4:13).

Jesus was not in the boat. The boys left him praying, doing his meditation thing. They wanted to "get up and get going." All was going well; they were singing "Row, row, row your boat; life is but a dream!" The wind kicked up, the waves got taller, and the ship was tossed. These guys were aware of the storms on the sea. Four of the twelve were pro fishermen. We wonder if Bartimaeus started getting seasick, if Judas "white-knuckled" the ministry purse, and if Thomas began doubting why he agreed to go along. They rowed for three and a half miles.

- Why did they not bring Jesus with them?
- Were they rowing with the wind or against the wind?
- When they raised the oars, did the wind push them backward?
- Or when one side of the boat rowed more than the others, did it send the boat off course?
- Were they just going in circles out in the middle in the dark?

The same is true with us. We use our own boat, our own strength, and our own friends. When we row in one direction alone, we find ourselves going in circles. We have to balance out our efforts. God sees us straining against the oars of life. He sees from the mountain. In fact, God sees us distancing ourselves from him, and at times he lets us go. Then, when bad weather comes our way, God rises and comes toward us.

Jesus walked on the water from the shore to the center of the lake. God not only turned water to wine at a wedding. Here he turned water into a walkway. Maybe you could have heard him whistling in the dark, walking toward the boat. He spoke words of comfort, and immediately they arrived where they wanted to go, this time with God beside them.

- Is Jesus in your boat right now?
- Or are you rowing with your own strength?
- Are you straining against the oars too?

PRAYER

God, I admit to the times I went it alone. I look back at the rough waters I went through, the times I strained to make things happen. I went backward. Today, maybe I am there. Would you leave your holy mountain and walk toward me in my direction? Please come to me, God; in my spinning in circles, I seek you and your peace.

WHEN GOD OFFENDS

"I am the bread of life. Your forefathers ate the manna in the desert, yet they died. But here is the bread that comes down from heaven, which a person may eat and not die. I am the living bread that came down from heaven. If anyone eats of this bread, that one will live forever. This bread is my flesh, which I will give for the life of the world." Then the Jews began to argue sharply among themselves, "How can this man give us his flesh to eat?" Jesus said to them, "I tell you the truth, unless you eat the flesh of the Son of Man and drink his blood, you have no life in you. Whoever eats my flesh and drinks my blood has eternal life, and I will raise that person up at the last day. For my flesh is real food and my blood is real drink ..." On hearing it, many of his disciples said, "This is a hard teaching. Who can accept it?" Aware that his disciples were grumbling

> about this, Jesus said to them, "Does this
> offend you?"
> —John 6:48–54, 66

What prevents us from following Jesus? Does his language offend? This speech about eating flesh and drinking blood stirred the listeners. It was graphic. It sounded gross. Why is that? Flesh-eating and blood-drinking are offensive. It was not conceptual language. It was table language, of feasting on the person of Jesus himself.

God would use communion to manifest himself later on a Thursday before his arrest and crucifixion. But here he transformed bread and a cup into his very own flesh and blood. It was one thing for Moses to transform the Red Sea into blood, but Jesus was going beyond that. It sent the scholars shuffling. And it offended the disciples, it seems—too close, too personal, unsafe.

If we want God to live within us, he asks us to digest his words and drink of his Spirit. And that offended then, and it offends so many today. God is polarizing.

- Can you share your faith in the corporate world?
- Do you have to be careful with expressing your belief system?
- How is tolerance diluting the witness of the church today, not in the sanctuary but in the office or classroom?

PRAYER

God, oftentimes I want you in my life, but I don't want you to get too close. Here in our reading I find myself scooting away from the table a bit. I prefer the calm, serene Communion service, the wafer on a silver tray and the wine, our juice, in the silver chalice. But here you are incarnational—in the flesh, blood poured. You bring me back to you on the cross, arms stretched taking my sins, looking down at me waiting for me to be real too.

NO LONGER
FOLLOWING

From this time many of his disciples turned
back and no longer followed him. "You do
not want to leave too, do you?" Jesus asked
the Twelve. Simon Peter answered him,
"Lord, to whom shall we go? You have the
words of eternal life. We believe and know
that you are the Holy One of God."
—John 6:66–69

When Jesus got too close and the attention went from the
miracles to the meal of the Messiah, many of his disciples
turned back. Note that these were not the distant ones
merely casting a glance at God. These were the students,
the ones who had walked behind him. They had invested
in his ministry. It was the disciples who turned back.

- How did Jesus feel as he saw them leave his mission?
- How did it feel for the disciples to turn away, to
  go back home or go follow another rabbi?

- Did any come back to Jesus before he went to the cross?

Jesus could not make everyone happy. Some chose to leave him. The one who walked on water, the one who healed the lepers—that one—could not satisfy some. Jesus in his sadness turned to see the people leave him. Then he turned back toward his Twelve and said, "You don't want to leave me too, do you?"

And then began the first game of Simon Says. "Lord, to whom shall we go? We believe. You are the One." Eleven out of the twelve would follow him to his death and resurrection. One did not.

Let's play the game of Simon Says. What he says we follow. But do we? Have you turned from God for a season or maybe a lifetime? What made you turn from God? Where are you now? Are you satisfied where you are? Do you agree with what Simon says? To whom shall we go if we depart from Jesus?

PRAYER

Have I left you, Jesus? Am I considering leaving you? What are my reasons? Where can I go to find hope and forgiveness? Simon would leave your side when you were arrested, but he jumped off his boat back to you later. How do you feel when people return to you after being away? Hear my silent prayer as I decide where I am right now in my relationship with you.

GET UP AND BRING IT

One day as Jesus was teaching, Pharisees and teachers of the law, who had come from every village of Galilee and from Judea and Jerusalem, were sitting there. And the power of the Lord was present for him to heal the sick. Some men came carrying a paralytic on a mat and tried to take him into the house to lay him before Jesus. When they could not find a way to do this because of the crowd, they went up on the roof and lowered him on his mat through the tiles into the middle of the crowd, right in front of Jesus. When Jesus saw their faith, he said, "Friend, your sins are forgiven."

—Luke 5:17–20

All the big dogs were there. The robed ones, the long beards, these were the Torah-keepers. The Pharisees had traveled on horses and donkeys, traversing the roads and navigating through the merchants soliciting their wares while the schoolchildren scampered through the city streets. These were the "separated ones." This is the first time they are mentioned in the Gospel of Luke. Six thousand Pharisees covered Palestine in that day according to historians. Their opposition to Jesus and his teachings and miracles was growing by the day. They were the vultures swooping in and closing in on the Christ, not to learn but to lean, not to hear but to jeer. They were hovering to lower the hammer on Jesus.

"Deadweight" is heavy. They had to rest, setting him down a couple of blocks away. One went ahead to survey the situation. They were late. The arena was sold out. They could have gone back, retracing their steps. The road back to their homes would be paved with good intentions. Jesus was busy, and he had a lot of people in line wanting to be near him. But did they give up? No. They had faith in their God, faith that they could find a way to get him to the feet of Jesus. They probably tried to force their way through the crowd whispering to each one in their way, "Coming through ... paralyzed man coming through." But they were blocked. Then one of them looked up. And they saw the roof, and the rest is history. They remembered that the stretcher was a ladder! Sometimes we have to be creative in our mission. There will be barriers and obstacles, and people will be in the way. But if we are persistent and invite others in bringing people to Jesus, big moments happen!

As he was speaking, the roof began to creak. Can you hear it? Men were peeling off the thatch to lower their friend to the feet of God. Jesus stopped speaking.

- What did he see? Did he see the paralytic?
- Did he see the tiles falling down around him and into his hair?

Jesus saw their faith. God saw what friendship looks like. Earlier that day, did the paralyzed man have any idea that God would enter his day? It was just another day bedridden in the middle of his nowhere. He went from being homebound to being holy bound! Jesus did not say much. But what he said was profound. He addressed him as "friend." And then he said what we all want to hear. "Friend, your sins are forgiven."

It all happened because a few friends joined together. They said "no" to disease and "yes" to the divine! They had responded to the whisper within: "Get up and go, get your buddy, and bring him to the Gentle Healer."

Maybe today you are outside of organized religion like this paralytic. Your compassion has not waned, just your taste for hypocrites. Today God sees you and how you love your friends. God sees your efforts to get connected spiritually. Maybe you are bringing a friend into the faith. God loves to see us share our faith with friends who might be lifeless. God takes the deadweight and brings us all back to life, healing us on the inside offering us forgiveness.

PRAYER

Stretcher-bearer I can be, God. I can tote. I am not much for public speaking, but I can lift a friend in silent prayer. I can take a family member to church who is in a wheelchair. I can go with her to the doctor's office or help her at the grocery store. I can do something today. I want to be like those friends. Or maybe I am the one on the pallet, needing you to call me "friend" and offer me forgiveness for my sins.

TAKE UP YOUR MAT

The Pharisees and the teachers of the law began thinking to themselves, "Who is this fellow who speaks blasphemy? Who can forgive sins but God alone?" Jesus knew what they were thinking and asked, "Why are you thinking these things in your hearts? Which is easier: to say, 'Your sins are forgiven,' or to say, 'Get up and walk'? But that you may know that the Son of Man has authority on earth to forgive sins …" He said to the paralyzed man, "I tell you, get up, take your mat and go home." Immediately he stood up in front of them, took what he had been lying on and went home praising God. Everyone was amazed and gave praise to God. They were filled with awe and said, "We have seen remarkable things today." —Luke 5:21–26

1. Jesus spoke to the Pharisees.

At first glance, it is easy to cast judgment. If a stranger who came out of nowhere arrived claiming to forgive sins, we might question it too. Throw in a miracle and strong teaching, and you have reason for jealousy and suspicion. "Who is this fellow?" Jesus was not in their fellowship.

- Who was this outsider who claimed to forgive sins?
- Where did he go to seminary?
- We did not see him at the academy library.

Notice that Jesus knew what they were thinking. He was a mind reader. They did not say anything out loud. Was it because they were scared of the crowd? God knew them, and God knew better. He knew their skepticism and was fully aware that he threatened their authority and power structures. Jesus spoke into their hearts. "Why are you thinking these things in your hearts?"

2. Jesus spoke to the paralytic.

"*Get up and go!* And take that mat, that thing you were lying on, and go home." What if you were in that house? You saw this paralyzed man jumping to his feet, reaching for that mat, and darting out the door down Sycamore Street. In his excitement, he could not wait to get home to show his family. Could you see him dancing, skipping, whistling, and rejoicing? In the faint distance, could you hear him singing the doxology? "Praise God from whom all blessings flow!"

If you were one of his friends, would you not run to his home alongside him? Jesus nodded at you, silently thanking you for making it possible. How did that make you feel? Your random act of kindness was recorded by Luke for all to read, even to this day.

Today, Jesus speaks to the Pharisee and the paralytic in each of us. We have both qualities. Maybe today you would like to take off casting judgment and put on the love and grace of Christ. Let's be Jesus to someone who needs forgiveness and healing. Christ is within you right now with the ability to move through you today!

PRAYER

God, wow! What a story of healing. Thank you for healing that guy. I love reading about you going up against the Pharisees, aware of what they were thinking. Nothing gets by you, God. I guess I need to be careful with my thoughts too, huh? You can do all things. Forgiveness gets me off my mat and back into life, dancing and rejoicing. I seek your forgiveness today. I am ready to show my family that I am a new person.

PROVIDENCE

Jesus went to a town called Nain, and his
disciples and a large crowd went along with
him. As he approached the town gate, a
dead person was being carried out—the
only son of his mother, and she was a widow.
—Luke 7:11–12

Jesus got up and went again. Here was Jesus the Creator in
carpenter's jeans with an entourage around him. He was
in the prime of his life. It was the season in his ministry
when he was popular. He was on his way to Nain, twenty-
five miles southwest of his Capernaum home.

For some reason, I imagine Jesus like Forrest Gump
running across the country … and people followed, aware
that he was different. Maybe you picture a civil rights
march as thousands of people joined step-by-step with
their leader. That is what we had here.

Did Jesus know what was waiting for him as he entered the
city limits? This was not just any funeral. It was a funeral

for the only son of a widow. Don't miss those words. An only son carried out of the city gates leaving behind his mother, who also was a widow. Sound familiar? A year later, Jesus would be carried out on a cross, killed outside the city gates leaving behind his mother, Mary. Joseph was not around or was deceased. At the scene was only a woman—a mother, a widow, grieving her son. Did Jesus recall this scene in Nain as he hung on that timber?

The "God moments" happen in the strangest of times and in the most unusual places. Do you have a recent experience when you came upon a scene that would shape you for the rest of your life? Sometimes it does seem like God plans these coincidences in our day, and if we are open to them, major things can occur.

Maybe coincidence is God incidence. What do you think about God's timing sometimes? How do you see the providence of God in your history?

PRAYER

Help me look for your timing today. Will I see parallels and possibilities to help me grow deeper in understanding of my purpose for living? Who will cross my path today that will deepen my understanding of your providence?

YOUNG MAN, GET UP!

When the Lord saw the widow, his heart
went out to her and he said, "Don't cry."
Then he went up and touched the coffin,
and those carrying it stood still. He said,
"Young man, I say to you, get up!" The
dead man sat up and began to talk and
Jesus gave him back to his mother. They
were all filled with awe and praised God.
"A great prophet has appeared among
us," they said. "God has come to help
his people." This news about Jesus spread
throughout Judea and the surrounding
country.
—Luke 7:13–17

This story in Nain seems so hard to believe. It's too easy
for Jesus. "Don't cry"? But this widow had had enough
loss, and now her son, her only begotten son, was dead.
All she could do was cry. But then he touched the coffin,
and the pallbearers stopped.

"Young man, I say to you, *get up*!"

What do you think the pallbearers thought? We all wish there was no more death and no more wailing. But death is part of life, and we all die. So why did Jesus heal this young man on that particular day? Who knows? We don't have the answer to that; perhaps he knew that this scene would be his scene soon. His mother would be crying beside the cross, wailing as the soldiers pinned him to the beam. Was he wondering about that, or was he having a "flash forward"?

All we do know is that this young man who was dead, was alive. What are times we have seen people who were lifeless come back to the joy of living?

- When someone who has been dead in addiction accepts words of forgiveness and turns toward wholeness, that person comes alive.
- Or a lonely person withdrawn from rejection is given attention; we have seen that person come to life.
- Or a person gets out of debt and is able to finally get up and get moving; we know what that looks like, right?

Resurrection comes in many forms and is all around us, if we will look for it. Miracles do happen. God is the one who speaks light into the dark and breathes life into the death chambers that encapsulate us all. So we can get up again, talk again, and be given back to our loved ones, just like this young man.

Have you ever had a resurrection experience? Have you been in a box and carried away, only to be given new life? Maybe you have been dead in the water or down for the count. And for some reason, you were given new air to breathe? Then you can relate to this story. Have you told anyone about it? Today is a good day to do just that!

PRAYER

You are the life and the resurrection, Jesus. I believe! I have seen people who were carried out in the pine box of pain and addiction and have been restored to healthy living. Please lift those who are like this widow in the wake of grief, a mother seeing her child suffer. I lift them to you now.

HOW TO SEE PEOPLE

> They came to Bethsaida, and some people brought a blind man and begged Jesus to touch him. He took the blind man by the hand and led him outside the village. When he had spit on the man's eyes and put his hands on him, Jesus asked, "Do you see anything?" He looked up and said, "I see people; they look like trees walking around." Once more Jesus put his hands on the man's eyes. Then his eyes were opened, his sight was restored, and he saw everything clearly. Jesus sent him home, saying, "Don't go into the village."
> —Mark 8:22–26

Healing takes time. It is a process for most of us. Very rarely do we go from being blind to seeing in a blink of an eye … or two. Are you going through a long season of cleansing? Then you can relate. Healing happens for most of us one day at a time. Maybe you are seeking to be healed of bad memories, or an infection, or a spirit of negativity. You know what ails you. How many days have you been in therapy or treatment? Today you can identify with this blind man. At this point in the story, he was still waiting to see clearly. And that is where most of us are today.

When Jesus touches us, we enter a new process of viewing people.

1. He saw people as objects.

He could see, but not clearly. He had blind spots. He said the people looked like walking trees. Sometimes we treat people as objects too. We see people for what they can do for us. It might be their fame or their image or their skills. The pornography business thrives on inviting us to see women and men merely as objects to satisfy our lusts. What other examples can you think of when we treat loved ones or strangers merely as things?

Jesus put his hands on the man's eyes again. This second time, his eyes were opened and his sight was restored. What did that mean? It meant that he saw everything clearly, just as the text stated. He saw people as people, not as objects.

2. He saw people as people.

Maybe you identify with this story in many ways. God requires we begin our mission with those who know us best. We have the opportunity to see them today with clear eyes and pure motives, not for what they can do for us. Would you like your family to see you that way too? What are our blind spots? How can Christ heal us today?

Jesus sent the man home. The first persons he needed to see were his family members. Maybe he would see them as God would see them—not as objects but as people created in the image of God.

PRAYER

Lord, I want to be more like you. You did not see people as objects. We are not merely a number to you. You know our name, you know our needs, and you meet us where we are. Please heal me today of my vision for life. Give me new eyes to see others around me, beginning in my home.

MAN CAVE

When Jesus came to the region of
Caesarea Philippi, he asked his disciples,
"Who do you say that the Son of Man is?"
—Matthew 16:13

Jesus told the boys to get up and go with him on a retreat
from one region to the next. The teaching lesson would
not come inside a building, a synagogue, or a home.
Jesus would use nature to create the theater; a cave would
become the backdrop.

Do you remember the image of the half horse, half man?
That is Pan. Scholars believe that in that cave would be
images of Pan and other gods such as Zeus. Surrounded
by those images and those who were worshipping there
and dancing around these gods, Jesus would stop the tour,
turn to his students, and ask them, "Who do people say
the Son of Man is?" In other words, "Who am I according
to your buddies and family members?"

Jesus did not ask that question in a sanctuary or a serene Sunday school room. He plopped them right smack-dab in the middle of pantheism and Greek mythology. It was Pan versus the Son of Man. Both were half and half. One played a flute seducing people into perversion. The other was man and God, playing a tune that brought pure joy, dancing at weddings, inviting people into purity. Where do we focus our attention as we peer into this cave? Pan is alluring, but the Son of Man ... there is something about him.

Jesus did his best work in the cave. Three caves for Christ: a borrowed cave at birth and a borrowed cave at death. And don't forget this cave. Who do people say Jesus is ... in the man cave?

PRAYER

Caesarea Philippi is still here. I find myself surrounded by other images of god. Pan is alive and well. Who are you, Son of Man? How do you compare with the allure of this culture, and do you inspire me outside my cave? I want to follow you, Son of Man ... but that flute playing around me is loud.

SAVIOR AND LORD

Jesus said to his disciples, "If anyone would come after me, that one must deny oneself and take one's cross and follow me. For whoever wants to save one's life will lose it, but whoever loses one's life for me will find it. What good will it be for a person if that one gains the whole world, yet forfeits one's soul? Or what can a person give in exchange for one's soul? For the Son of Man is going to come in his Father's glory with his angels, and then he will reward each person according to what that person has done."
—Matthew 16:24–27

Discipleship has two phases:

1. *Jesus is Savior.* We come unto Jesus and fall at the foot of the cross. We see what he did for us by taking our place. He paid the ransom note for our sins so we could be reconciled to God the Father.

He saved us from eternal death and offers us life forevermore. We come to Jesus as Savior. We ask him to forgive our sins so we may live with him in heaven.

2. *Jesus is Lord.* After we come to him as Savior, we come after him so he can be Lord. We are his disciples. We learn to follow the leader. God is in charge, and he wants to be part of every decision we make each day. Jesus is the guide on the mountain trek, the one who blazes the new trail in the woods, and he takes us into the city to see how we spend our time, our talents, and our money.

It is not easy to relinquish the reins when you are accustomed to being in charge. But if we want to save our lives, then it is best if we lose them. Look around at the graspers. We have plenty of people in our lives who are trying to grip life and hold on. Buy one more sweater, get that pair of jeans while they are sale, and get so consumed with things that we get cluttered and unable to move around our house or closet.

- Doesn't this leave us bankrupt, broke, and begging for relief, strangling on the stress, seeking relief?
- Have you been there? Have you sold out to the consumeristic model too?
- Have you gotten tired of your old things and so had a garage sale, basically giving it all away,

making a dime out of every dollar you spent on it all? And then what?

- We go and buy more! Why is that?

God offers another way of living. Deny self, take up the cross, and follow Jesus. Every morning before our feet hit the floor, we have to decide. Every invitation we get to go out at night, we have to discern. Maybe you have been gaining the whole world but forfeiting your soul? Join the club.

PRAYER

God, today I get to decide if you will be my Savior and my Lord. It is easy to receive you as my Savior because it is clear that you have done the work to reconcile me to God. But to receive you as my Lord is another matter. It demands conversation and conversion. Where am I today in my discipleship? Am I following you with my stewardship? Am I consumed out, chasing the almighty dollar? You invite me to *get up and go* be your disciple today. Hear my earnest prayer now ...

RAZZLE-DAZZLE

> After six days Jesus took with him Peter,
> James and John the brother of James,
> and led them up a high mountain by
> themselves. There Jesus was transfigured
> before them. His face shone like the sun,
> and his clothes became white as the light.
> —Matthew 17:1, 2

A week has passed since Jesus asked his disciples to come
after Jesus, deny self, take up their cross, and follow him.
Now Jesus invited three of them to join him on a hike. It
was a holy hike away from the other nine disciples. Do
you wonder what the others were thinking? They were not
invited to join Jesus. Have you ever been left at the bottom
while others were elevated? Of course you have. Imagine
how Andrew felt. He was the one who had introduced
his brother, Simon Peter. And yet it was Peter who was
tapped on the shoulder to climb with Christ.

They started low and went high. The trio triumphed with
Jesus from the plateau to the pinnacle.

- Were they scared? Were they puffed up with pride?
- Did they shrug their shoulders when they looked back at the other disciples?
- Did they feel guilty for being selected when the others were not?
- What would it have been like to have been chosen specifically by Jesus?
- How would you feel? How would you respond?

They were led to a private place all "by themselves." These were fishermen far away from the familiar waters. They were not mountain climbers. They preferred boat shoes to hiking boots. God invited them to get up and go with him, and they followed. They had no idea where Jesus was leading them. But they walked in his footsteps then and for the rest of their lives.

It would be a Messianic metamorphosis, the caterpillar coming out of the cocoon. His face lit up, and his clothes beamed. This Palestinian peasant was the Prince of Peace. It was the culminating moment, from Christmas to the carpenter's shop where he had served for so many years. It was because he *got up and went* from his woodworking business to share the Gospel. This was his time to prepare for the final days ahead. He would need reassurance about his mission to earth. How would he receive it?

God the Father poured out his unimaginable glory onto his Son. He bathed his boy in majesty, transforming him like Moses was when he talked with Yahweh. Jesus would shine, and the fishermen saw his face shining like the sun and his clothes white as the light.

As you pray, consider this image of Jesus today. See the face of Jesus on this mountain blazing like the sun and white in purity, covered in light. View your prayer life as a daily journey up the holy mountain to see God in all his glory. Bask in his light, and feel the warmth of his love. Let's *get up and go* and see some razzle-dazzle!

PRAYER

Jesus, oh to see you in your majesty one day. Until then, thank you for this glimpse into your glory today. May you be transfigured from a historical figure to the holy figure called to change the world one person at a time. Hear my prayer, oh Lord.

@NOON

Jesus had to go through Samaria. So he came to a town in Samaria called Sychar, near the plot of ground Jacob had given to his son Joseph. Jacob's well was there, and Jesus, tired as he was from the journey, sat down by the well. It was about noon. When a Samaritan woman came to draw water, Jesus said to her, "Will you give me a drink?" His disciples had gone into the town to buy food. The Samaritan woman said to him, "You are a Jew and I am a Samaritan woman. How can you ask me for a drink?" (For Jews did not associate with Samaritans.) Jesus answered her, "If you knew the gift of God and who it is that asks you for a drink, you would have asked him and he would have given you living water." "Sir," the woman said, "you have nothing to draw with and the well is deep. Where can you get this living water? Are you greater than our father Jacob, who gave us the well and drank from it himself, as did also his sons and his flocks and herds?" Jesus answered, "Everyone who drinks this water will be thirsty again, but whoever drinks the water I give will never thirst. Indeed the water I give will become a spring of water welling up to eternal life." The woman said to him, "Sir, give me this water so that I won't get thirsty and have to keep coming here to draw water." He told her, "Go, call your husband and come back." "I have no husband," she replied. Jesus said to her, "You are right when you say you have no husband. The fact is, you have had five husbands, and the man you now have is not your husband. What you have just said is quite true …" The woman said, "I know that Messiah is coming. When he comes, he will explain everything to us." Then Jesus declared, "I who speak to you am he."

—John 4:4–18, 25–26

Who told her to *get up and go* to the well at high noon? She had no idea that on that particular day, she would meet God. Did she go at the hottest part of the Judean day to avoid people? Did she mumble to herself about the poor choices she had made in her life or ask God why she had been through so many marriages? As she arrived at that well, she would have to confront another man. She did not have good luck with men.

Of all people to whom Jesus would admit to being the Son of God, he shared it with this Samaritan woman. What an honor for this dishonorable lady. She had been married more times than you could count on one hand, and she was shacking up with another. Of all people to have a chance encounter with God, it was this woman of scandal.

- Have you had a chance encounter with a stranger that would change your view on an issue or inspire you when you least expected it?
- Think of those times when your path crossed with another who would shape you more than you realized.
- Where did you see God today?

Imagine this Samaritan woman telling you her story.

PRAYER

I would like to refresh you with my prayer life today, God, for you must be tired from your journey. Thank you for taking my past history and still meeting me at the well today!

JESUS OR THE JAR

Just then his disciples returned and were surprised to find him talking with a woman. But no one asked, "What do you want?" or "Why are you talking with her?" Then, leaving her water jar, the woman went back to the town and said to the people, "Come, see a man who told me everything I ever did. Could this be the Christ?" They came out of the town and made their way toward him.
—John 4:27–30

Peter and the boys came bursting on the stage not realizing what had just happened. A woman's life, that of a no-named woman whose sins had caught up with her, was being transformed. While they were at the market, she was offering water to God without knowing it. And in return, he offered her "living water" and told her all about her own life, her shame, and her scorn. Despite her past, because she was honest about it, God blessed her.

She bolted from the scene, and she left behind the water jar. The very thing that had been a part of her daily existence, her major chore, she left behind. She came to fill up on *Jacob* water, but she left filled up on *Jesus* water! She was alive! And she danced toward her friends at home, and they all wanted to see Jesus for themselves.

- Do our lives attract others who want to know this God who is making a difference in our lives?
- Are we drinking the living water or settling for counterfeits that make us groggy, more thirsty, or even hungover?
- Have we shared cold water with Jesus without even knowing it?

The jar or Jesus—which is it for us?

PRAYER

Lord, I want to drink of this living water and to leave behind my water jar. I am tired of toting it. It is my burden. I fill it up with what the world offers, and it is breaking my back and my spirit. The daily chores of life are killing me. Please offer me a deeper meaning to my life today. I want to be alive too.

LET HIM GO

Jesus, once more deeply moved, came to the tomb. It was a cave with a stone laid across the entrance. "Take away the stone," he said. "But, Lord," said Martha, the sister of the dead man, "by this time there is a bad odor, for he has been there four days." Then Jesus said, "Did I not tell you that if you believed, you would see the glory of God?" So they took away the stone. Then Jesus looked up and said, "Father, I thank you that you have heard me. I knew that you always hear me, but I said this for the benefit of the people standing here, that they may believe that you sent me." When he had said this, Jesus called in a loud voice, "Lazarus, come out!" The dead man came out, his hands and feet wrapped with strips of linen, and a cloth around his face. Jesus said to them, "Take off the grave clothes and let him go."

—John 11:38–44

We eavesdrop on Jesus praying to his Father. He said words for the benefit of those around him—so that they would know what? So that they would believe that God sent Jesus. It is all about the sending.

1. Jesus was fully human. He was deeply moved. Jesus wept at the tomb of his best friend, Lazarus. He ate fish, drank wine, danced at weddings, drank water from a well, told stories, and prayed prayers. Perhaps that is what makes you fall in love with Jesus. It is his relational style of living. He was the perfect man with the best personality and, yes, a sense of humor to go along with common sense. He was a storyteller, a healer, a fisherman, and a shepherd. Jesus was human.

2. Jesus was fully divine. While Martha was worried that Lazarus was rotting away inside that cave, Jesus was ready for Lazarus to rise again out of that cave. He had the godly ability to believe the impossible and tried his best to bring Martha along with him. As God spoke life out of the dark in Genesis, so Jesus spoke words of life out of the dark in this Gospel. With God, all things are possible indeed.

How do you see Jesus in this story? He showed what it is like to be fully human with all the emotions and also to be fully capable of performing the greatest miracle of all—bringing someone who has been dead for days back to life.

Jesus told Lazarus to *get up and go*. And he did. "Lazarus, come out!" And as soon as he emerged, what did Jesus say? He wanted Lazarus to lose the grave clothes, the things that tangled him and reminded him of his death. He wanted him unbound and set free. Jesus said the ultimate words: "Let him ... go." Do you wonder if they had a party?

- What are the grave clothes that are binding you and preventing you from living?
- What in your past is holding you down or holding you back?

PRAYER

Jesus, what a story! It is the Easter story for Lazarus! Today will you call me by my name and tell me to come out of my darkness toward you? I am ready to be sent outward!

EASTER DARK

Early on the first day of the week, while it was still dark, Mary Magdalene went to the tomb and saw that the stone had been removed from the entrance. So she came running to Simon Peter and the other disciples, the one Jesus loved, and said, "They have taken the Lord out of the tomb, and we don't know where they have put him!"
—John 20:1–2

Easter happened for Mary because while it was still dark, she would *get up and go*. She was the one accustomed to the dark. Years earlier, she'd been eaten up with darkness, and Jesus had healed her. As a result, she followed Jesus everywhere after that healing. She lit a torch, and into the dark she went—to grieve, to weep, to remember.

My preference for observing Easter is for people to come into a church *not* with all the lilies in place and the lights on and the joyful music playing. I prefer to work through the Easter morning with Mary Magdalene, to enter a dark sanctuary like it is a funeral, perhaps being lit by a single torch. Allow the drama to unfold as Mary reminisced. What was she thinking? Why did she get up so early? Could she not sleep? She was at the foot of the cross. She was there when they took the nails out of his hands after he died. She was there when Joseph of Arimathea donated his tomb for Jesus. She was probably there when they buried him. Let's stay with Mary in the dark at Easter. It is powerful.

While it was still dark, something else happened. God the Father tiptoed past the Roman guard, and with the angels pushing back the stone, the Dad went in to breathe life into his Son. It all happened … in the dark.

- How do you imagine the resurrection happening?
- Was it immediate or gradual as Jesus came back to life?
- What did Jesus think as he opened his eyes and reached for his hands?
- Did he feel the wounds? Where did he go after coming out of the grave?

Are you afraid of the dark? Are you frightened of death? Take heart today. God does his best work in the dark. He came for his only begotten, and he comes for those who feel forgotten.

PRAYER

Jesus, what was it like to be dead and buried and on the third day to rise again? What was the first thing you saw out of the Easter darkness?

MARY'S MISSION

Then the disciples went back to their homes, but Mary stood outside the tomb crying. As she wept, she bent over to look into the tomb and saw two angels in white, seated where Jesus' body had been, one at the head and the other at the foot. They asked her, "Woman, why are you crying?" "They have taken my Lord away," she said, "and I don't know where they have put him." At this, she turned around and saw Jesus standing there, but she did not realize it was Jesus. "Woman," he said, "why are you crying? Who is it you are looking for?" Thinking he was the gardener, she said, "Sir, if you have carried him away, tell me where you have put him, and I will get him." Jesus said to her, "Mary." She turned toward him and cried out in Aramaic, "Rabboni" which means Teacher. Jesus said "Do not hold on to me, for I have not yet returned to the

Father. Go instead to my brothers and tell them, 'I am returning to my Father and your Father, to my God and your God.'"
Mary Magdalene went to the disciples with the news: "I have seen the Lord!" And she told them that he had said these things to her.
—John 20:10–18

Let's highlight two missional points in this Easter story.

1. The Church can hold Jesus back from his mission.

The Easter Jesus was ready to *get up and go*. He did not want Mary to hold on to him, because she might never let go. What people slow down the mission of God? It is not the unbelievers who could care less; it is the church that tries to hold Jesus for itself. "God so loved the world"—not "God so loved the church."

Mary wanted to preserve the moment; Jesus was ready to get moving. For days he had been dead and buried. He was ready to come out of the dark into the Easter light and add more to the church!

2. Mary first went to the disciples; then the disciples went into the world.

Jesus told her to get up and go where? He sent her on a mission to tell the church that Jesus was alive. You would think Jesus would send her to those in Jerusalem, perhaps

Pontius Pilate or Herod or the soldiers who nailed him to that cross to tell them that Jesus was alive and ready to take revenge! But her mission was to go to the disciples and tell them what she had seen. She was to be the first witness to take the stand and tell the truth, the whole truth, and nothing but the truth. She got up and went. She told them. And from that day to today we recite this story at Easter and have to ask if we in the church believe today.

- If we in the church do not believe, then why should they on the outside believe?
- And if we believe, unbelievers want to know what the Easter story means in our daily lives.
- Where will you see God today? That will be your Easter story!

PRAYER

Lord, as much as I want to keep you to myself, I understand that your mission is ongoing. Send me on my mission, perhaps to tell my church friends again the good news of the Easter story and why it is important. It is my hope on earth as it is in heaven. You are the Redeemer, the one who conquered death. Because you live, I will live also—now and later!

GET
UP
and
GO
with the Apostles

DON'T GO YET!

On one occasion, while he was eating
with them, he gave them this command:
"Do not leave Jerusalem, but wait for the
gift my Father promised, which you have
heard me speak about. For John baptized
with water, but in a few days you will be
baptized with the Holy Spirit."
—Acts 1:4–5

We begin a new series after Jesus was resurrected. We will
walk with the early church to see how they were called and
sent to serve. Before Jesus ascended into heaven, he left
behind some important words that would determine the
future of faith. If they disobeyed, the mission of Christ
would have ended. But if they obeyed, the mission would
grow one generation at a time. For weeks he remained
with his disciples to get up and go. But here he said
something different.

"Do not leave Jerusalem."

But they wanted to leave. They were exhausted, scared, and ready to go back to the Sea of Galilee. Their leader had been crucified, and they feared they would be next. Jerusalem was the scene of the crime. But now they were to stay in Jerusalem because they were in need of something very important.

What was the gift that the Father had promised them? It was the Holy Spirit, the third person of the Trinity. The Spirit would guide them along their way. They could not imagine life without Jesus. So he offered to put Jesus into their hearts. Did they comprehend what he meant? It was doubtful. Days later, they would understand what he meant, but at that table that day, they simply heard the command.

The most important gear that a missionary needs is the Holy Spirit. We need the indwelling of Christ within our hearts and minds. Without it, we might go on our own strength. Then what? God offers us the strength of God to keep going upward and outward in the Spirit of Christ.

Wait. Stay in your Jerusalem until you are baptized in the Holy Spirit, immersed in God's grace, covered in the holy, surrounded by the living water, and bathed in forgiveness.

Would you like to receive the Holy Spirit now? He promises to fill you to the brim!

PRAYER

Lord, I want to serve you, but don't let me bolt out of here today before I ask for your Holy Spirit for this day. I will wait for you, though it is not so easy to wait …

FIVE VERBS OF THE HOLY SPIRIT

So when they met together, they asked him, "Lord, are you at this time going to restore the kingdom of Israel?" He said to them, "It is not for you to know the times or dates the Father has set by his own authority. But you will receive power when the Holy Spirit comes on you."
—Acts 1:6–8

"Is it time, Lord?" It was a good question, but it was a political one. They were ready for their Messiah to topple Caesar. They were zealots, trapped in the empire, every street corner with an armed soldier to remind them they were surrounded. They were ready to be set free from those Romans, who had strung up their God, nailing him, spearing him, and gambling for his clothes.

His answer would be his final words on earth. "Don't focus on the future. Live in the present!" Receive the gift of the Holy Spirit to power up and truly live in the present moment. When we invite God into our lives, the Holy Spirit will empower us to explode with joy and purpose. The word *power* is the same word for *dynamite*. It can blow away walls of hatred and mountains of distrust. The church would become a missile, and they would need the fuel to explode and expand!

Here is a simple way to remember five verbs of the Holy Spirit. Hold up your hand.

1. *Convicts* us. (Hold up your pointer finger.) We need the finger of God to point into our chest to change our hearts. Oftentimes the Spirit challenges us so we can be more like Christ.
2. *Converts* us. (Hold up two fingers like a peace sign.) God oftentimes gives us a person to help change us along the way. It takes two people in the journey.
3. *Cleanses* us. (Hold up three fingers.) We are baptized in the water of the triune God: Father, the Son, and the Holy Spirit.
4. *Comforts* us. (Pop up your pinkie like you are drinking from a cup of tea.) God provides the Comforter to keep us warm and out of the cold.
5. *Controls* us. (Hold up your thumb.) God has his thumb on us to control our movement as we mature in the faith.

Questions we might ask as we seek to grow closer to God are

- Have you experienced the tweaking of the Spirit to improve your life?
- Have you converted your power source to him?
- Would you like to be cleaned up?
- Do you need warmth in this cold world?
- Would you like help to be controlled by the God who loves you and has big plans for you?

Is it time, Lord? What is preventing me from asking for your Spirit today?

PRAYER

Yes, God, power me up. Plug me in! I want to be wired for sound, with a full battery to serve. Get me fired up, God. Hear my prayer as I ask for the Holy Spirit, the person of Jesus, to live within me.

FOUR MISSION FIELDS

> You will be my witnesses in Jerusalem,
> and in all Judea and Samaria, and to the
> ends of the earth.
> —Acts 1:8

The Greek word for witness is *martus*, from which we get the word *martyr*. A martyr is a person who is willing to die for telling his or her testimony. A witness takes the stand to tell the truth, the whole truth, and nothing but the truth. Sometimes it might cost people their lives.

Let's look at the progression of the missionary's journey.

1. Begin at home. That is Jerusalem.
2. Go into your community. That is Judea.
3. Go outside your comfort zone. That is Samaria.
4. Go beyond. That is to the ends of your world.

We share the good news in everyday conversations in the grocery story, visiting nursing homes, in the bleachers, and over a cup of coffee with a friend. As we mature in faith, God will naturally send us farther out. We are asked to be witnesses to what God is doing around us. Are we willing to take a stand against bullies, theft, and hatred in the name of Christ?

- Jerusalem: Who in your home needs words of encouragement?
- Judea: Who in your neighborhood needs care and compassion?
- Samaria: Who outside your local community needs a helping hand?
- Ends of the Earth: Where is God calling you that you never imagined God would send you?

Where is your Jerusalem, your Judea, your Samaria, and the ends of your world?

Each of those disciples would become a martyr. A dozen disciples went on a mission to change the world. And they spread Christianity in the power of the Holy Spirit! Because they did, we are here today.

PRAYER

I prefer the "witness protection" service, God. If I was willing to tell others what you were doing in my life, people would think I was a "Jesus freak." And for too long, Lord, I have been quiet. I am tired of being quiet. I want the power of the Holy Spirit to be bold. Send me to my home first and then beyond. Let's get up and go, God! Let's change the world!

DEPARTURE TIME

After he said this, he was taken up before
their very eyes, and a cloud hid him from
their sight.
—Acts 1:9

He went from the scars to the stars. Jesus was restored!
He was transitioning between this world and the next.
He flew home. Jesus had accomplished his mission—to
be the incarnation, God in the flesh, an atoning sacrifice
for the sins of the world. He created the church by calling
twelve disciples, shaping them by teaching and miracles
and meals, and sending them in the power of the Spirit to
continue God's mission of love and serving others.

The baton was passed. God would rely on average people
to *get up and go* spread the good news. His strategy for
the planet was to plant Gospel seeds along the roads and
paths of everyday life. Jesus was called back to where he
was before his Christmas incarnation in that stable with
Mary and Joseph. He was sent upward with the angels
and at home with Dad.

This was the ultimate *get up and go* experience. His work on earth was complete. The doors opened in heaven, and God the Father was pacing the floor eager to see his Son. Picture that homecoming. Imagine as the angels were dancing, choirs were singing, and Moses and Elijah were at the gates waiting for the King of Kings. Picture the arrival at the gate, and see the reunion as Jesus was running to his Father, whose arms were opened wide!

There is a departure time for each of us.

- Can you envision your departure from this earth and the welcome that awaits you in your future?
- Have you quit imagining? If so, why?

PRAYER

Jesus, what were you thinking as you looked at your departure time waiting to finally get home to your Father? Talk about homesick! I love how you went home. You walked on water before. But then you walked on air. Nothing was impossible for you. The grave could not hold you. You were alive! You lifted your arms, raised your eyes, and were home. I look forward to meeting you one day.

KEEPING US GROUNDED

> They were looking intently up into the sky as he was going, when suddenly two men dressed in white stood beside them. "'Men of Galilee," they said, "why do you stand here looking into the sky? The same Jesus, who has been taken from you into heaven, will come back in the same way you have seen him go into heaven."
>
> —Acts 1:10–11

What if we were standing there beside the apostles? We stopped, we looked intently, and our mouths were open. We could not move. All we could do was stand there and gaze. The Son of Man, the coolest carpenter's kid, the gentle healer, the one who turned ordinary people into leaders, and who transformed the blind to see, the deaf to hear, the lame to walk, and the dead to rise was rising not just from the dead, but rising before our eyes to heaven.

Notice the angels did not hover in the sky like they did with the shepherds at Jesus's birth. No, these men dressed in white "stood beside them." Appearing out of nowhere, the boundary between heaven and earth was merged. The Messiah flew to heaven, but the heavenly presence descended to the disciples. One got up and went upward; the two angels got up and went down. Can you see the stairway between heaven and earth? They passed each other along their way!

The disciples were looking at the sky. God had taken these men, who were so focused on their businesses as fishermen or tax accountants or whatever they were doing. He offered them the big picture of life. The final scene involved everyone looking upward. The steeples on every corner in your town or city invite you to look upward into the sky, to remember this moment when Jesus was sent to his throne room, where he is Lord of Lords and King of Kings.

In the same way he went into heaven, Jesus will come back one day for a final *get up and go*. The trumpet will blow, and all the earth will be restored to God as nations and people will stand before God, giving an account of how they used their time to be in mission.

The temptation for the "men of Galilee" was to look at the pie in the sky. They could marvel and reminisce of the good ol' days, of yesteryear when they began following Jesus. But the angels woke them from their trance and reminded them that life goes on.

This was no pie-in-the-sky theology. The angels said, "Get moving in mission!"

PRAYER

God, it is easier to see the pie in the sky than to see the homeless and needy, the orphans and widows who need me. Keep me grounded, God, and while I look forward to heaven, may I bring a little heaven on earth.

HOLY SPIRIT TIME

> When the day of Pentecost came, they were all together in one place. Suddenly the sound like the blowing of a violent wind came from heaven and filled the whole house where they were sitting. They saw what seemed to be tongues of fire that separated and came to rest on each of them. All of them were filled with the Holy Spirit and began to speak in other languages as the Spirit enabled them.
> —Acts 2:1–4

Fifty days after Easter and following the ascension of Jesus into heaven, the people remained all together in one place. In Genesis 11, the people were together too, and they decided to build a tower and a name for themselves. They had the same language, but unfortunately they began to build not for God but for their own pride. God confused their language, and the place would be called the Tower of Babel.

But this time the people could understand one another. From all over the world, they did not need a translator. They could speak like never before, and there was universal unity. God brought them together, and the rush of a mighty wind filled the place and a tongue of fire rested on each of them. They were filled with the Spirit of Jesus Christ!

When we are in the Spirit, we have chemistry, communication, and community. Do you have that in your office or classroom? What about your team or in your club?

- Have we felt the wind blow the staleness out of our lives?
- Has the Spirit rested on us?
- Are we in the place where God is moving, or are we far off? It is Holy Spirit time!

PRAYER

God, I want this Holy Spirit, the wind of God, to blow freshness into my heart and mind. I seek fresh air, the breeze of blessing so I may be filled to love more deeply. Keep me in community, and lead me into deep worship of you, the God of compassion and commission.

RISE AND SHINE

Now there were staying in Jerusalem God-fearing Jews from every nation under heaven. When they heard this sound, a crowd came together in bewilderment, because each one heard them speaking in his own language. Utterly amazed, they asked: "Are not all these who are speaking Galileans? Then how is it that each of us hears them in his own native language? We hear them declaring the wonders of God in our own tongues!" Amazed and perplexed, they asked one another, "What does this mean?" Some, however, made fun of them and said, "They have had too much wine." Then Peter stood up with the Eleven, raised his voice and addressed the crowd: "Fellow Jews and all of you who live in Jerusalem, let me explain this to you; listen carefully to what I say. These men are not drunk, as you suppose. It's only nine in the morning! No, this is what was spoken in the prophet Joel: 'In the last days, God says, I will pour out my Spirit on all people. Your sons and daughters will prophesy, your young men will see visions, your old men will dream dreams. And everyone who calls on the name of the Lord will be saved.'"

—Acts 2:5–8, 11–17, 21

It was time for Simon Peter to rise to the occasion. This was the one who had denied Jesus three times after Jesus was arrested. After Christ's death and resurrection, Jesus met Simon Peter by the Sea of Galilee and restored him again to lead. Can you hear him as he cleared his throat and explained the marvel of the movement of the wind and the unity of language in that upper room? We watched as he got up and spoke from his heart.

What a first sentence to his sermon! "These men are not drunk, as you suppose. It's only nine in the morning!" The people must have acted drunk, filled with joy and perhaps dancing around that room! They were filled with the new wine of the Spirit, of celebrating oneness in God. They were not slurring their speech but were speaking clearly of the wonders of God. It was God-speech with Christ as the subject of their sentences and the theme of their conversations.

The Holy Spirit fell on the church, and there was an aliveness that drew the crowd to ask what was happening. The church was kindled from a spark to a blaze.

- Is our church on fire for God?
- Is the language centered on God or on other things?

Today, crowds of people are looking at the church as a whole. What do they see, and what do they hear? How is the church offering opportunities for members to share what God is doing in their lives? It is time to rise and shine!

PRAYER

Oh, to be a fly on the wall in that upper room, swept by the Spirit, listening to the words. What would it have been like to see a wounded disciple named Peter get up and respond to those who were making fun of them? Thank you, God, for Peter and for restoring him and forgiving him so he could serve in a mighty way. Restore me today that I may serve you and speak of your wonders. Fire me up, God!

THE SIMPLE GOSPEL

Jesus of Nazareth was a man accredited by God to you by miracles, wonders and signs, which God did among you through him, as you yourselves know. This man was handed over to you by God's set purpose and foreknowledge; and you, with the help of wicked men, put him to death by nailing him to the cross. But God raised him from the dead, freeing him from the agony of death, because it was impossible for death to keep its hold on him ... God has raised this Jesus to life, and we are all witnesses to the fact. Exalted to the right hand of God, he has received from the Father the promised Holy Spirit and has poured out what you now see and hear.

—Acts 2:22–24, 33

Simon was standing up to be counted. From limestone to granite, from petrified to Petrus (meaning Rock), Peter became the leader of the early church. He was the first to take the witness stand and speak the whole truth, including the fact that people in that room were the very ones who had condemned Jesus to be crucified.

There were no politically correct speech here, no tiptoeing, no hiding the white elephant in the upper room. Peter the rock, whose name used to be Simon, was chiseled by heartache himself, all too familiar with how he had participated in the passion of the Christ and denied that he knew Jesus by the courtyard fire awhile back. Now he had the fire within him and the bold Holy Spirit that was in Jesus!

He succinctly shared the Gospel. He described the life and death and resurrection of Jesus. God raised Jesus from the agony of death, and death could not contain him. God is always "out of the box," and God had commissioned Simon Peter to "fish for people." Finally, he was doing it here on Pentecost! He cast his net over the people there with his words of conviction.

- Can we share the Gospel story in a simple way?
- Have we ever shared the story of Jesus with someone?

Perhaps today we will be invited to share our love for God. He loves to hear his name brought up in our conversations. Maybe we will even share the Gospel story!

PRAYER

Jesus, your miracles, your wonders and signs ... let me reflect on some of them now. And let me see you as you poured out your heart for us on the cross. You were raised from the lifeless, because death in all its coldness and grasp could not keep its hold on you. Thank you for the resurrection, God! Send me today, God, to weave your wonders into my schedule—I pray.

ALL-INCLUSIVE

"Therefore let all Israel be assured of this: God has made this Jesus, whom you crucified, both Lord and Christ." When the people heard this, they were cut to the heart and said to Peter and the other apostles, "Brothers, what shall we do?" Peter replied, "Repent and be baptized, every one of you, in the name of Jesus Christ for the forgiveness of your sins. And you will receive the gift of the Holy Spirit. The promise is for you and your children, and for all who are far off—for all whom the Lord our God will call."
—Acts 2:36–39

The people wanted to know what to do. They were cut to the heart and recognized their sins. So Peter offered what every church today offers—a chance to turn around and to wash off the dirt and decay of the past, to come out of the waters and receive the Holy Spirit of mission.

This promise was not just for adults but for families—husbands, wives, children, grandparents!

The upper room became an "all-inclusive" resort, not for the holy but for the ones with holes in their hearts! The price has been paid in one lump sum ahead of our arrival.

- Would we like to be set free from the decay and filth of our lives?
- Are we ready to wash the stains out of our lives?
- Is it time to receive the Spirit that comforts inwardly so we can be commissioned outwardly?

When we go to a worship service, it is more than checking it off our list of weekly things to do. It is also more than shaking the hand of the minister and going to our cars. Worship leads us to ask the following questions:

1. How does this Gospel propel me to respond, to act, to move, to be sent as Christ into the world?

2. How can I be a light in the dark, or salt that offers taste in a bland culture?

The Gospel is especially for those of us who are far off. Maybe you are there right now.

Welcome to Sandals Resort, where we walk in the footprints of the one who wore the sandals of salvation. You don't need to bring your credit card. It has all been paid in full. Enjoy the resort even if it is your last resort to find joy. You've come to the right place!

PRAYER

Before I get on the plane to come to the resort, I am a bit scared of what it means to ask you into my heart. I want to turn from my destructive ways and some secret sins, and to be immersed in your warm waters of renewal. Will I lose my personality? Will I no longer have fun? I feel far off, but I thank you for coming to those who are far away, distanced but seeking you.

TAKING THE PLUNGE

> With many other words he warned
> them; and he pleaded with them, "Save
> yourselves from this corrupt generation."
> Those who accepted his message were
> baptized, and about three thousand were
> added to their number that day.
> —Acts 2:40–41

Christianity spread one person at a time. It still does. Jesus
invited Andrew. Andrew invited Simon. Three years later
Simon would invite this big crowd! The church went from
a few to three thousand all in one sermon! That is the
power of the Gospel. It is not boring, and it engages each
listener to make a decision. Do I follow self or a Savior?

What a banner day for God, and what a first birthday
of the church! Can you imagine seeing thousands of
people baptized—plunging into the river, lined up for
miles, waiting their turn ... to turn. People were ready to
improve, to be scrubbed clean, and come out of that river
renewed and refreshed in the Spirit. They could not help

but go share what had happened to them. It was natural growth, one conversation at a time. That is the pattern, the rhythm of a church that is alive.

- When was your baptismal pool or font last used in your church?
- Has it been a while?

Baptism is the sacrament at the entrance of the church. It is the font of beginnings, the waters of discovery, the pouring of the Spirit available to each of us right now. Have you been baptized yet?

"Come on in; the water's fine!" These words from the movie *O Brother, Where Art Thou?* echo in my ears as I picture an escaped prisoner inviting his friends into the waters of forgiveness. He immediately invited his buddies to join him. One did; the other did not. The choice was up to each one, just like in our passage. Which do you choose? Are you ready to *get up and go* and make a splash?

PRAYER

God, where am I in my relationship with you? Do I want to be washed clean of my sins? They are ever before me. Blot out my transgressions—I pray. I want to join you in the river of righteousness. I'm ready to take the plunge!

THREE IN THE AFTERNOON

> One day Peter and John were going up to
> the temple at the time of prayer—at three
> in the afternoon. Now a man crippled
> from birth was being carried to the temple
> gate called Beautiful, where he was put
> every day to beg from those going into the
> temple courts.
> —Acts 3:1–2

It was months after Easter Sunday. The two guys who
were together then were still a team. Jesus in his ministry
had sent the disciples to heal and teach in pairs. Jesus
used these two Galileans, extreme opposites, the original
"odd couple," to share the Gospel together. John was the
thinker, and Peter was the talker. Together they would be
hooked at the hip with the holy calling. Both fishermen,
they were called to "fish for people" in the big city of
Jerusalem, far from the shores of Capernaum.

They were going into church at three o'clock in the afternoon. Why would Luke include this detail in the story? It was the same time of day that Jesus breathed his last breath on the cross. As the school camels were letting the kids off from school, and as merchants were hard at work, the bell rang for holy worship. It was gathering time physically and mentally, the time to get centered. Peter and John sensed the call to go worship in a temple.

At the same time, a crippled man was placed at the gate called Beautiful. He was propped up there with a bowl and a sign that said, "Help me." How do you picture him? He was not beautiful. This no-named beggar was crippled, perhaps with a cane beside him. He had been that way all his life, from birth to now. He felt displaced, disowned, and in disarray. Every day they placed him by the gate called Beautiful.

- Which character are you in this story?
- Are you the disciple or the deserted?
- Do we identify with the healthy or the unhealthy?
- If God sent you as a disciple today, who would be your partner in mission?
- How do we treat beggars? Do we avert our eyes and pretend they are not there?

Today you might meet a man who is at the exit ramp on your way home. It is three o'clock in the afternoon. His sign reads,

I'm Hungry. Please Help Me.

Do you mumble under your breath something about the lazy poor? How do you know if his plea is legitimate or a scam? How do you discern when to help and when to hold back?

PRAYER

Jesus, how would you treat the poor if you were in my shoes today?

JUMPING FOR JOY

When the crippled beggar saw Peter and John about to enter, he asked them for money. Peter looked straight at him, as did John. Then Peter said, "Look at us!" So the man gave them his attention, expecting to get something from them. Then Peter said, "Silver or gold I do not have, but what I have I give you. In the name of Jesus Christ of Nazareth, walk." Taking him by the right hand, he helped him up, and instantly the man's feet and ankles became strong. He jumped to his feet and began to walk. Then he went with them into the temple courts, walking and jumping, and praising God. When all the people saw him walking and praising God, they recognized him as the same man who used to sit begging at the temple gate called Beautiful, and they were filled with wonder and amazement at what had happened to him.

—Acts 3:3–10

Beggars make us feel uncomfortable, forcing us to ask what we have and what they do not have. They make us realize how fortunate we are. But they also can play off our guilt. So oftentimes, we dig into our pockets and purses and give money out of obligation. Other times we give out of compassion. Sometimes we care. Sometimes we do not.

Peter and John were heading to worship. Little did they realize that the real worship experience would happen before they would enter the synagogue! The crippled beggar, who was placed at the gate called Beautiful, in all his poverty and pain and brokenness, would become the sermon himself.

Peter looked straight at him, and so did John. They did not avert their eyes away from the poor. They zeroed in on the beggar, his legs splayed in a crippled fashion. But the beggar was not looking at the apostles. He was merely shouting for money, and Peter and John were just two in the line amidst others. His plea was not personal; it was a blanket statement.

He was looking away, or maybe … he was looking down, embarrassed, ashamed.

Peter said, "Look at us!" So the beggar raised his face and his eyes to the ones over him. But he looked only because perhaps he expected to get something from them. Little did he know that what they would give him would change his life forever!

Peter offered not money but the Messiah. What the no-named beggar really needed, money could not provide. He had no hope of ever walking. In fact, he had never walked before. He had been crippled since birth. We imagine he wanted to skip, to run, to dance, to embrace his wife and his children and grandchildren. He wanted to throw away that cane and end the days of relying on others to place him at that gate. But when did that hope give way to giving up?

Peter dared to boldly witness to the healing power of Jesus. Peter offered him the same thing that got him off his duff after he had denied Jesus three times. As Jesus came to him and restored him by the shores of Galilee, now Peter got to pay it forward.

He would offer two aspects of a missionary's calling.

1. Speech: He said nothing about himself. It was all about God. "In the name of Jesus Christ of Nazareth, walk." *Get up and go!*

2. Outreach: He extended his hand, felt the weight of the crippled man, and used his leverage. The right hand in scripture is a symbol of strength, power, and determination. There was power in physical touch. Peter had seen it every day when he was with Jesus as Jesus touched the crippled and the lame.

What happened? He jumped to his feet. He sprung upward from hearing the words in the name of Christ. He jumped at the chance to go and worship! Imagine that!

A friend was diagnosed with cancer. It changed his outlook on his relationship with God. He decided as long as he was alive, he would go to church. He would put the clothes he would wear on Sunday on the bed Saturday night. He was preparing. In other words, he was excited about worship. Cancer had caused him to jump at the chance to worship … just like this beggar by the gate called Beautiful. Through Christ, he was beautiful again!

PRAYER

Wow! What a story, God. It is one thing for Jesus to heal, but Peter? The fisherman who was more used to mending his nets than to mending crippled legs? Is it possible for others to heal? Today I am that beggar. I look upward and ask you to speak words of healing, and take me by the right hand so I can jump to my feet and join others in the fullness of life!

FLABBERGASTED
BY FAITH

While the beggar held on to Peter and
John, all the people were astonished and
came running to them in the place called
Solomon's Colonnade. When Peter saw
this, he said to them: "Men of Israel, why
does this surprise you? Why do you stare
at us as if by our own power or godliness
we had made this man walk? The God
of Abraham, Isaac and Jacob, the God
of our fathers, has glorified his servant
Jesus. You handed him over to be killed,
and you disowned him before Pilate,
though he had decided to let him go. You
disowned the Holy and Righteous One
and asked that a murderer be released
to you. You killed the author of life, but
God raised him from the dead. We are
witnesses of this. By faith in the name of
Jesus, this man whom you see and know

was made strong. It is Jesus' name and
the faith that comes through him that has
given this complete healing to him, as you
can all see."
—Acts 3:11–16

The beggar had his arms around John and Peter, vertical
and seeing others eye-to-eye for the first time. He was
whole, well, and no longer that cripple by the gate called
Beautiful.

The miracle was part one. But the telling of the story was
part two. When we see a miracle, the temptation is to
focus on the person who received that miracle. And that
is good; yet it is not the complete story. We need to give
credit to the one who healed. It is not the physician or the
stranger alone who came alongside the person who was
hurting. It included God.

His testimony blistered those who were there. Peter let
them have it. He reminded them of what they did to Jesus.
They helped to arrest him, beat him, and hand him over
to Pontius Pilate. They asked for Barabbas to be released
instead of Jesus. Peter was still stinging with anger. He
was on the witness stand speaking his mind, no longer
cowering by the courtyard fire. He was filled with the
fire of faith-speech.

Though Jesus was not around physically, speaking in his
name brought healing.

- Do we believe that God can heal through the words and witness of disciples?
- If God can move mountains with the mustard seed of faith, then when it happens, why do we drop our jaws in amazement?
- Have you heard of or witnessed a healing?
- Were you flabbergasted too?

PRAYER

I admit it, God. While I pray for healing, when it happens, I cannot believe it. I too am astonished when I hear that a tumor is gone. I find myself wanting to believe, but then, when good things happen, I wonder why I ever doubted. Is it natural to be skeptical, to be real? A crippled beggar who was able to jump up all of a sudden is astonishing. I believe. Help my unbelief.

THE ONE CHURCH

All the believers were one in heart and mind. No one claimed that any of his possessions were his own, but they shared everything they had. With great power the apostles continued to testify to the resurrection of the Lord Jesus, and much grace was upon them all. There were no needy persons among them. For from time to time those who owned lands or houses sold them, brought the money from the sales and put it at the apostles' feet, and it was distributed to anyone who had need. Joseph, a Levite from Cyprus, whom the apostles called Barnabas (which means Son of Encouragement), sold a field he owned and brought the money and put it at the apostles' feet.
—Acts 4:32–37

The Nicene Creed says we believe in the one holy catholic (universal) church. We witness this fact in the passage above. They were one. They were holy in their understanding that all of life is a gift. They were expanding their universe beyond the homogenous beginnings. The church was growing in members and mission.

Stewardship is a fancy word for paying it forward. Sharing what we have with others is the response we have when Jesus gets our hearts. We begin to move from greed to grace. Possessions no longer "possess" us. We join the early church and demonstrate love by distributing our resources within the community.

The church was becoming the welfare department, and that is why it grew so quickly. They were a missional church, sending members into the mission field to see how their property and their homes and their excesses could be sold so the money could become a tool and a testimony for sharing that Christ was alive.

- Is there a widow or widower who needs help in our community?
- Is there someone who has trouble paying his or her power or water bill?
- Have you ever been a recipient of such a gift?

Today we are challenged to get up and go, and take an inventory of our excesses and how we can share, and pay it forward. That is what it means to be in a missional church. Would you like to be a member of that kind of church today?

PRAYER

When I look at my portfolio of stocks, bonds, and cash or open my garage to see my vehicles or look out the window at my land, it is tempting to say to myself, "I worked hard for this. It is mine." At the end of our lives, we cannot take it with us. There is "no pocket in the shroud." Remind me of that today, Lord. How can I share in the here and now? Who has shared with me when I have been in need? I pause to give thanks for them.

THREE LESSONS
ON MONEY

Now a man named Ananias, together with his wife Sapphira, also sold a piece of property. With his wife's full knowledge he kept back part of the money for himself, but brought the rest and put it at the apostles' feet. Then Peter said, "Ananias, how is it that Satan has so filled your heart that you have lied to the Holy Spirit and have kept for yourself some of the money you received for the land? Didn't it belong to you before it was sold? And after it was sold, wasn't the money at your disposal? What made you think of doing such a thing? You have not lied to people but to God." When Ananias heard this, he fell down and died. And great fear seized all who heard what had happened. Then the young men came forward, wrapped

up his body, and carried him out and
buried him.
—Acts 5:1–6

Here we meet a couple who had good intentions, but
along the way they got greedy. It happens to the best of
us. When we get the cold cash in our hand, it has the
potential to make us make cold decisions. We can either
share the benefits with others or hoard it. We can open
our hands or close them. Look at all the lottery winners.
Have you seen how money has the potential to actually
destroy people's lives? Why is that?

This couple knew what they were doing was wrong in the
eyes of God. They held back. Peter, representing God, saw
that the money they brought was not the full price of the
sold property. Notice his language. He focused in on how
stewardship is a spiritual matter.

Ananias was the first "Slinky." Remember that toy? It
was a spring that could be placed on a stair and when
let go, it would go down. Ananias was at the top stair of
stewardship, selling his land, doing the right thing. But
the next thing he knew he was descending down the stairs
in greed. How quickly money can change our direction if
we are not careful.

There are at least three uses of money:

1. Money is a *test*. It will reveal character and
    integrity.

2. Money is a *tool*. It can fix the broke and repair the broken.
3. Money is a *testimony*. It reveals our motives and our mission.

Ananias died that day from his poor decision of stewardship. So do we when we let greed get in the way of our good intentions. Let's take an inventory of what we do with our paychecks. What percentage do we share? It is a testimony indeed of what we value as important! Maybe it is time to buy a Slinky.

PRAYER

God, as I look at my financial life, how am I "holding back" like Ananias and Sapphira did? What can I learn from their story? I agree that I die on the inside when I hoard and grip and hold on for dear life. Help me, Lord, to remember that all I have is yours …

A WIDOW'S MIGHT

About three hours later his wife came in, not knowing what had happened. Peter asked her, "Tell me, is this the price you and Ananias got for the land?" "Yes," she said, "that is the price." Peter said to her, "How could you agree to test the Spirit of the Lord? Look! The feet of the men who buried your husband are at the door, and they will carry you out also." At that moment she fell down at his feet and died. Then the young men came in and, finding her dead, carried her out and buried her beside her husband. Great fear seized the whole church and all who heard about these events.

—Acts 5:7–11

The expression "widow's mite" comes from the story of Jesus watching people bringing their tithes to the front in a worship service. He said that people would remember a widow who gave a mite (pennies) because others gave out of their abundance. She gave out of her poverty (Mark 12:41-44).

This is the story of a widow's might. She exercised her power not to give but to grab. As a result, she died. It's a comedic moment in scripture that might remind us of the Keystone Cops. The young men had carried out her dead husband, and then three hours later, they rushed back in with a stretcher and carried out the dead wife.

Marriages live and die by money. When we have money, we can easily purchase. And purchases can lead to clutter and worry. Sometimes we get to the point that we cannot enjoy the things around us, because they need maintenance and upkeep. It exhausts us, and before long we wonder if it is worth keeping. Have you gotten to that point? Would you like to find peace, or would you like to hold on to what you have and grasp for more? When we share what we have, it opens us to a new way of living. The early church offered the chance for people to give to the needy. The church offers the same today. There comes a time to simplify our lives.

Pull out a piece of paper. Jot down your worries. How many of those worries revolve around money? As we balance our checkbooks, let us balance between grace and greed.

PRAYER

Today I reflect on what I give to charity and the church. This text haunts me as it makes me review my priorities of my possessions. Am I truthful? Do I rationalize my purchases and pride myself on the things around me? Curb my enthusiasm to buy more and more. Instead, let me look around and see what I have and how I can relinquish control so you may be glorified. Do I need to simplify my life today?

HELP WANTED

In those days when the number of
disciples was increasing, the Grecian
Jews among them complained against the
Hebraic Jews because their widows were
being overlooked in the daily distribution
of food. So the Twelve gathered all the
disciples together and said, "It would not
be right for us to neglect the ministry
of the word of God in order to wait on
tables. Brothers, choose seven men from
among you who are known to be full of
the Spirit and wisdom. We will turn this
responsibility over to them and will give
our attention to prayer and the ministry
of the word." This proposal pleased the
whole group. They chose Stephen, a
man full of faith and of the Holy Spirit;
also Philip, Procorus, Nicanor, Timon,
Parmenas, and Nicolas from Antioch, a
convert to Judaism. They presented these
men to the apostles who prayed and laid

their hands on them. So the word of God spread. The number of disciples in Jerusalem increased rapidly, and a large number of priests became obedient to the faith.

—Acts 6:1–7

The word in Chinese for crisis is also the same word for opportunity. The leadership in the early church expanded because of a crisis in food management. There was division in the ranks between the Greek widows and the Hebrew widows. One side felt snubbed with the Meals on Wheels program, and the twelve were overwhelmed trying to manage everything. The twelve could have chosen to be the managers of the church for their lifetimes. Why not? They were the ones handpicked by God himself in Jesus to create the church. But what did they do? They delegated. That is leadership.

Enter the creation of church deacons. The Greek word for deacon (*diakonos*) means "waiting at tables." Deacon ministry is being sent out of the kitchen to serve others. The church chose seven people (holy number of completeness) who were full of Spirit and wisdom. These seven were selected to offer servant leadership just as Jesus did at the Last Supper (John 13).

Maybe you feel like a deacon, called to "wait at tables." Behind the scenes, you are more into action than words. The church grows when more and more people are invited into ministry!

On a mission trip to Brazil down the Amazon River in a triple-decker boat, each missionary worked a night in the boiling-hot kitchen preparing the meal and cleaning up after the meal. We each gained a new perspective on the kitchen workers who worked tirelessly without fanfare to minister to our team. As I look back on that trip, I realize that I learned as much about God on the boat as I did in the villages. I saw deacon ministry at its finest.

God puts out the sign today: "Help Wanted. Deacons Needed." Are you in?

PRAYER

Lord God, I focus today on the little things behind the scenes. Can I bring in a grocery cart still in the parking lot? Or take a meal to a homebound friend? How can I serve with you today as a deacon, not rushing but waiting ... on tables?

TAKE CARE

As Peter traveled about the country, he
went to visit the saints in Lydda. There he
found a man named Aeneas, a paralytic
who had been bedridden for eight years.
"Aeneas," Peter said to him, "Jesus Christ
heals you. Get up and take care of your
mat." Immediately Aeneas got up. All
those who lived in Lydda and Sharon saw
him and turned to the Lord.
—Acts 9:32–35

It is the story of lost and found. Peter first found the
paralytic. Where did he find him? He was not begging
beside a road or sitting beside a pool. He was bedridden.
He had been in that same spot for eight long years. For
almost a decade he had had to rely on others to get him
bathed and fed. We picture Peter kneeling down beside
the bed.

Did Peter have a flashback to all those times when he
saw Jesus perform miracles? Did he recall the time the

paralytic was lowered through the roof and Jesus healed him with words? Peter said the exact same words. "Get up and take care of your mat." But first he said, "Jesus Christ heals you." In other words, it is not I who heals but Jesus.

"Jesus Christ heals you."

It sounded so simple. The one who had ridden a bed for so long was able to ride a camel. How could this be? We wish it happened like that today. The truth is, God works in mysterious ways. Some are healed physically, and others are healed mentally and spiritually. But the point was that God finds us where we are. And we are invited to "get up and take care."

What is our mat? God says to take care of it.

- Take care of your health.
- Take care of your home.
- Take care of your business.
- Take care of your family, your friends, and your pets.
- And take care of your soul.

God says to get off the mat, get active, and allow others to see us alive in the Spirit. People just might see us and turn to the Lord. Get up and take care of yourself! God loves you!

PRAYER

I hear your words today. I will get up and go. I will take up my mat and walk! I will take care of myself and those around me with your strength and in your Spirit.

GET UP AND GO TO SAMARIA

Those who had been scattered preached the word wherever they went. Philip went down to a city in Samaria and proclaimed the Christ there. When the crowds heard Philip and saw the miraculous signs he did, they all paid close attention to what he said. With shrieks, evil spirits came out of many, and many paralytics and cripples were healed. So there was great joy in that city.
—Acts 8:4–8

"Who wants to *get up and go* spread the Gospel to Samaria?" All you could hear were crickets. No Jewish disciple wanted to go to the enemy camp of Samaria. Samaritans were people with a checkered history. They were called "half-breeds" who intermarried and blended foreign gods with Yahweh. They were not pure like these Jews. This was the attitude despite the fact that oftentimes in Jesus's parables, it was the Samaritans who were the heroes. And despite Jesus's giving living water to a Samaritan woman a while back, nobody wanted to go to Samaria.

Except one, the deacon named Philip. Maybe they all drew straws, and guess who got the short one? But he went faithfully, boldly sharing the Gospel. Did he expect the people to be receptive to him? Philip was a Greek Jew, and he was different from the Samaritans. And yet they saw the miracles and "paid close attention to what he said." His words mattered. They shaped lives, and in the name of Jesus Christ he was even able to heal those with crippling pasts. Philip was a hero.

- Is there a Philip that you know who is willing to go across enemy lines and simply share the good news of God's hope and mercy? Perhaps the line is not far. It might be within your home.
- Or maybe it is a missionary who serves in the Congo around people with AIDS or a soldier sent to Iraq to be a peacekeeper.

In every mission, we are called to cross over lines meant to divide. Maybe that person is you. You know your Samaria. And God is showing you great signs of his presence there now. Do you see joy in Samaria? Maybe it happened because you brought it.

PRAYER

Thank you for Philip. Send me to a tough place today, and let's share the Gospel together in word, in deed, and in love. Move me beyond Jerusalem across my invisible borders.

TO BE ENTERTAINED

Now for some time a man named Simon had practiced sorcery in the city and amazed all the people of Samaria. He boasted that he was someone great, and all the people, both high and low, gave him their attention and exclaimed, "This man is the divine power known as the Great Power." They followed him because he had amazed them for a long time with his magic. But when they believed Philip as he preached the good news of the kingdom of God and the name of Jesus Christ, they were baptized, both men and women. Simon himself believed and was baptized. And he followed Philip everywhere, astonished by the great signs and miracles he saw.

—Acts 8:9–13

In this corner we have the Great Entertainer, and in this corner we have the Dynamic Deacon! It was Simon versus

Philip. Simon had the greatest show on earth until Philip showed up. Then Simon lost his audience. Philip did not claim to be great; instead he proclaimed the greatness of God.

He was seen walking back and forth into the river, baptizing these people and sharing the Gospel. He came to Simon and invited him into the water. We will see in the next devotional what happened to Simon, but this was when he began learning the difficult lesson of following God.

What entertains us today? We are surrounded by pyrotechnics and smoke and mirrors, from Grammy Award shows to the Super Bowl halftime shows. Maybe it is a gadget, a phone app, that new thing that draws us in and makes us want it no matter the cost.

- What in culture is competing with the Gospel presentation of Jesus today?
- Can the Gospel story compete today?
- How is the church responding to today's cultural shifts from words to images?

The temptation is to go to church … to be entertained. We need to pay attention to this text. Whom do we worship? Simon the magician is alive and well.

PRAYER

Lord, it is a daily struggle to choose Christ over the bright images of advertising. Their marketing techniques are drawing us, and we are entertained. We are amazed at the technology around us and available to us. How can the Gospel entertain me today? Or is that the purpose of the miracles and messages? Maybe it is not to entertain me, but to engage me into mission ...

WE'VE GOT SPIRIT

> When the apostles in Jerusalem heard that Samaria had accepted the word of God, they sent Peter and John to them. When they arrived, they prayed for them that they might receive the Holy Spirit, because the Holy Spirit had not yet come upon any of them; they had simply been baptized into the name of the Lord Jesus. Then Peter and John placed their hands on them, and they received the Holy Spirit.
> —Acts 8:14–17

Peter and the boys had to be scratching their heads. It was one thing for Israel to accept the word of God, but for Samaria to say *yes* to Jesus was amazing. So Peter and John packed their bags; they were called *to get up and go* to Samaria and see the ministry of a deacon named Philip.

The church headquarters were behind the times of what God was doing outside Jerusalem. That is common. The local church is where the movement of God usually begins, and it takes time for the denomination to hear. But when they hear, they want to be a part of the action, and that is fantastic!

When Peter and John arrived, they saw God was moving mightily. Then they offered more of the story of God. They shared about the Holy Spirit and retold stories of Jesus and his ministry. All was good in Samaria, and the people received the Spirit of Christ in their hearts. The movement was expanding as the apostles were expounding! Things were unfolding just as Jesus had promised (Acts 1:4–8).

Here are some questions that arise as we read this passage:

1. If the Spirit can succeed in Samaria, can the Spirit not minister anywhere?
2. Is there a place where we deny God can move today? It might be around the corner, or it might be in a country with radical terrorism.
3. Is there a section of town that seems to be overrun by crime and where there is no turning back?
4. Can people who were walking in darkness see the light and yield to Jesus Christ today?

PRAYER

As I reflect on these questions, hear my thoughts and my prayers. Where do I fit in to your plan for sharing the Spirit with those in the dark?

BUYING GOD

When Simon saw that the Spirit was given at the laying on of the apostles' hands, he offered them money and said, "Give me also this ability so that everyone on whom I lay my hands may receive the Holy Spirit." Peter answered, "May your money perish with you, because you thought you could buy the gift of God with money! You have no part or share in this ministry, because your heart is not right before God. Repent of this wickedness and pray to the Lord. Perhaps he will forgive you for having such a thought in your heart. For I see that you are full of bitterness and captive to sin." Then Simon answered, "Pray to the Lord for me so that nothing you have said may happen to me."
—Acts 8:18–25

Simon was a famous entertainer in Samaria, yet he was drawn into the ministry by Philip. Simon would be baptized, and yet he still wanted to be entertained by God. He saw what happened when his audience received the Holy Spirit by another Simon named Peter. Sensational Simon met Simple Simon. Simon the magician reached for his checkbook. He offered to buy the Holy Spirit. He tried to bargain with God.

In this day and age, we can be tempted to use our stewardship to bargain with God. If we write a big check for a charity or church, we will be recognized. We have to be careful, don't we? It is tempting to buy our way into heaven, to tithe with the wrong motives, to share so our names can be on a plaque or a stadium.

- How do we use our resources to further mission?
- Is stewardship a dangerous enterprise if we get off course and focus on what we do with "our" money?
- What are some lessons you see in this passage today?

Judas sold Jesus to the Pharisees for thirty shekels, the price of a slave. What price would you put on God today if you could buy God? What is he worth to you?

PRAYER

Before I condemn Simon the magician, this is a good time to look at my own motives for sharing my resources. Speak to me in the stillness of this time, and shape me with purity and passion for mission.

IN BETWEEN

> Now an angel of the Lord said to Philip, "Get up and go towards the south (at high noon) to the road that goes down from Jerusalem to Gaza. This is a wilderness road."
> —Acts 8:26 (NRSV)

Deacon Philip was called in Jerusalem and scattered to Samaria, where he faithfully shared the Gospel and healed many people. It would have been easy for him to relax, to coast, and to see retirement in his future. He was well-known, well-respected, and at the top of his game. But just when he perhaps was getting comfortable, we read the familiar words: "Get up and go." But where would God lead Philip?

1. Get up and go on a deserted road into the wild at high noon.

The road often leads us into the deserted, the barren, the empty wasteland. It was not a road used very often. It was off the beaten path. Why would God call a missionary there?

Philip was called at high noon, the same time that the Samaritan woman met Jesus that day beside Jacob's well (John 4). It was the same time that Jesus was suspended on the cross between the curses of criminals and the earthquake later in the day.

The call into mission is out of the ordinary oftentimes, and we end up at a place that appears to be nowhere. But nowhere is also two words: now here. Did Philip ask for more clarity or better directions? Would you have wanted to know more about the mission before going? Surely he deserved more! He was the only one who agreed to start a ministry in Samaria, where even the apostles refused to go at the beginning. They were scared, but Philip was not!

2. Get up and go between.

It was a call to go from Jerusalem to Gaza. That was it. He was not asked to go to Gaza. He was asked to simply walk the road between the two cities. What a strange mission.

- Where is your road in between?
- Are you in transition today?

Maybe God is calling somebody to meet you today, to encourage you along your way. It will be a walk on the wild side when all you have is a sense of being driven beyond. God simply asks us to *get up and go* at lunchtime to a particular restaurant or to a specific table in the school cafeteria. God will tell you what to do next. Just follow!

PRAYER

How am I in between today? Some of my friends are also in between relationships or careers or neighborhoods or cities. We are all in between home and work, work and play. Speak to me and call me, Lord, to get up and go on this road where you are directing me today, trusting that there is a purpose in my being there.

INTO THE GAPS

So he got up and went. Now there was
an Ethiopian eunuch, a court official of
the Candace, queen of the Ethiopians,
in charge of her entire treasury. He had
come to Jerusalem to worship.
—Acts 8:27 (NRSV)

Philip was called to get up and go down a boring road.
Or so he thought. He went between Jerusalem and Gaza,
not an exciting road but a desert road, a wilderness road.
It was barren and seemed to be absolutely in the middle
of nowhere. At the same time, another person was on
that same road. This person was African, unable to have
children, and the queen's treasurer. He was coming home
from worship in Jerusalem.

God brought these two totally different people together
on that road. Philip was a Greek, and this man was
Ethiopian. Philip was able to get close to the holy of holies
in the Jerusalem temple, but this eunuch could not. The
eunuch's body was mutilated, which prevented him from

getting close to the holy. He was sent to the nosebleed section. Yet this eunuch was searching for the holy in his life. He was turned away.

- Did Philip know at that moment that God had called him there for that one person? Or did he first just want to walk by the stranger and not engage him in conversation? What would the missionary do?
- Who are the people who are turned away from organized religion today? Who are the seekers who might feel cut off from the faith yet are still striving to discover God in their lives?
- Are we sent into the gaps like Philip? If so, where is God leading us?

PRAYER

Who are the seekers around me today? They might not look or act like I do. But does that matter? Will I associate only with those who are like me? Will I engage or disengage? Will I be curious about their story, or will I be more concerned with mine?

LESSONS FROM PHILIP

> He had come to Jerusalem to worship and was returning home; seated in his chariot, he was reading the prophet Isaiah. Then the Spirit said to Philip, "Go over to this chariot and join it." So Philip ran up to it and heard him reading the prophet Isaiah. He asked him, "Do you understand what you are reading?" He replied, "How can I, unless someone guides me?" And he invited Philip to get in and sit beside him.
> —Acts 8:27–29

What can we learn about ministry in this story? God offered two whispers to Philip. The first call to Philip was in Samaria for him to *get up and go* from there down south on a dusty road between Jerusalem and Gaza. He got up and went and came upon that stranger. The second call was to not run from the stranger, but to *go* over to the chariot and join it. How did he follow God's direction?

1. Philip *saw* the person. He was Ethiopian, he was a eunuch, and he was the queen's own treasurer. Picture the rims, the brass, the tapestries draped over the rails. Philip saw a student feeding on the meal on wheels. He saw a seeker who, despite being sent to the back courts of the temple, was still wanting to learn as much as he could about God.
2. Philip *listened*. He heard scripture, and he knew it came from the suffering servant passage of Isaiah 53.
3. Philip *asked* a question. "Do you understand what you are reading?"
4. Philip *waited* to be invited to share the Gospel.

What can we glean from this narrative? We are to look at people and learn their stories. We are to listen, then ask questions, and wait to be invited to share our faith in God. Today, the missionary is to stay near the fast-moving chariot of culture. Discipleship does not begin with answers, but with questions.

Notice the seeker's answer. It would be a pathway for sharing the story of God. "How can I unless someone guides me?" A teacher might stay in a classroom, but a guide is willing to go where the people are asking questions.

- Are you a trail guide ready to go where God is leading you?

- Would you like to be around more people outside the church and discover the questions they have?
- Then be a Philip and run toward that chariot today!

PRAYER

May I model today what I learned in this passage. Help me to be a missionary like Philip, to see people, to listen to their stories, to be near, and to wait for an opening to share God's hope and healing. Or maybe I need a Philip to guide me today along my path on my road in between. Speak to me, Lord, through this scripture—I pray.

FROM BAD TO GOOD

The eunuch was reading this passage of Scripture: "He was led like a sheep to the slaughter and as a lamb before the shearer is silent, so he did not open his mouth. In his humiliation he was deprived of justice. Who can speak of his descendants? For his life was taken from the earth." The eunuch asked Philip, "Tell me, please, who is the prophet talking about, himself or someone else?" Then Philip began with that very passage of Scripture and told him the good news about Jesus.
—Acts 8:32–35

Do you want the good news or the bad news first? That question is what we imagine as we hear the seeker reading the suffering servant passage from Isaiah 53. The seeker did not understand. He was reading about Jesus being a sacrifice like a lamb before his shearer. It was about the death of Jesus, not Isaiah. It was about the crucifixion of a coming Messiah.

Philip began with that very passage and moved on from there. What appeared as bad news of Jesus dying was actually good news for us. It was the Good Friday message as God reconciled us to himself through Jesus on the cross. In the short term the cross is bad news. Jesus of Nazareth died a cruel death. But in the long term the cross is good news. It became a bridge for us to cross from self to service, from me to mission. Philip took the bad news of death and used it as good news, the Gospel to invite this eunuch to follow God. We saw a conversion taking place, not on the road to Damascus or the Emmaus road, but the road in between.

- Which person are you in this story? Are you the seeker or the server?
- Who is leading you to understand God's words for your life? Is it a teacher, a coach, a spouse, a child?
- Perhaps you will be led by a stranger who is eager to take you where you are and move you further in God's design in outreach and ministry.

Thank you for these two strangers united by the Spirit of God, talking deeply about what mattered in life because they were willing to *get up and go*!

PRAYER

Am I the seeker in this story? Am I seeking a guide to help me understand? Who is a mentor, a trail guide to help me on my journey? Or am I the guide today?

FROM SCARED TO SACRED

As they traveled along the road, they came to some water and the eunuch said, "Look, here is water. Why shouldn't I be baptized?" And he gave orders to stop the chariot. Then both Philip and the eunuch went down into the water, and Philip baptized him. When they came up out of the water, the Spirit of the Lord suddenly took Philip away, and the eunuch did not see him again, but went on his way rejoicing. Philip, however, appeared at Azotus and traveled about, preaching the gospel in all the towns until he reached Caesarea.
—Acts 8:36–39

Water appeared out of the desert! The drama unfolded with each turn of the chariot wheels. Picture God's excitement as he enabled the story of his Son to be shared beyond Jerusalem and Samaria! Here it was going to travel to a place it had not gone before … to Africa.

Once the Gospel was shared, it invoked a response. The seeker wanted to belong. Baptism was that symbol. Perhaps Philip was talking about the sacraments of the Lord's table and the sacrament of baptism. Just then, out of nowhere appeared water. "Look, here is water. Why shouldn't I be baptized?" Together they went into the water, an Ethiopian and a Greek celebrating the oneness they had through Christ. The eunuch went home, where legend has it he shared the Gospel in Ethiopia. All of it happened because two people were doing their best to love God and love their neighbor.

Today, there are many like this eunuch in our midst. We all have our cuts and scars and wounds. Many people have been cut off in life and wounded by the faith community. We often are scared. And that is when God brings us to a person to offer the sacred. Notice that these words have the same letters. They look alike but are so far apart. Maybe that is where we are. We are scared. And, like this eunuch, we too are scarred. God is offering us the sacred in the street beyond the sanctuary. The Gospel is for all who are cut off from community because of their past. Just ask this eunuch.

PRAYER

Where are my scars? When am I scared? Where can I find the sacred today? Listen to my prayers, Lord.

OUR DAMASCUS ROAD

> Meanwhile, Saul was still breathing out murderous threats against the Lord's disciples. He went to the high priest and asked him for letters to the synagogues in Damascus, so that if he found any there who belonged to the Way, whether men or women, he might take them as prisoners to Jerusalem. As he neared Damascus on his journey, suddenly a light from heaven flashed around him. He fell to the ground and heard a voice say to him, "Saul, Saul, why do you persecute me?" "Who are you, Lord?" Saul asked. "I am Jesus, whom you are persecuting," he replied. "Now get up and go into the city, and you will be told what you must do."
>
> —Acts 9:1–6

At the same time Philip was on the road in between, Saul was on the road to Damascus. This is another "get up and go" moment in history, which would shape Saul's future and ours too. Saul was on a rant—a righteous rant, he thought. His zeal for the Jewish faith gave him the rationale that it was all right for him to murder and imprison these new believers in the church called "The Way."

As he neared Damascus, but was not there yet—in that middle ground—a light went off around him. He was knocked to the ground to humble him. And then Jesus told him to get up and go into Damascus.

- Has God knocked you down yet?
- If you have gone in the wrong direction spiritually, has God forced you to fall?
- Who around you is a modern-day Saul?

God told Saul to *get up and go* into the city and wait.

PRAYER

Sometimes, God, you have to knock me to the ground to get my attention. You won't leave me on the mat, but you will tell me to get up and go again with humility. When was a recent time when the light came on around me and I realized that I was not as great as I thought I was?

BLIND SPOTS

The men traveling with Saul stood there speechless; they heard the sound but did not see anyone. Saul got up from the ground, but when he opened his eyes he could see nothing. So they led him by the hand into Damascus. For three days he was blind, and did not eat or drink anything.
—Acts 9:7–9

Blind spots. Every vehicle has blind spots that the driver has to be aware of. Where are they? The back right corner and behind the left shoulder of the driver. They are the narrow areas that keep us from seeing completely around us. This guy had it all—the pedigree, the position, the power—yet he too had his blind spots. He could not see the new picture of how Jesus had fulfilled the Old Testament and was living in New Testament times. Can you envision Saul as he was led by the hand into the very city where he intended to send new Christians to prison? Here he was the one imprisoned. He could not eat. He could not drink. That is grief. He was at a loss for words. He lost more than his sight. He lost his pride. The man who had the vision to kill all converts had blind spots to the grace of God in Jesus Christ.

This passage demands that we think about our own lives.

- What are our blind spots?
- Are we irrational at times?
- Do we have prejudices that keep us from seeing the bigger picture of life?
- How have we become haughty? Why does God have to keep humbling us?

Today, God is leading us by the hand into our own Damascus, ready to teach us lessons that will transform our lives. God did not leave Saul on that road to die alone. He kept him in community, around people, and they would teach him more than he could imagine. The same is true with us!

PRAYER

Where are my blind spots, Lord? Who are the people in my life who are there with me in my dark days? I pause now to remember them and thank you for those who hold my hand and lead me forward ...

GET UP AND GO, ANANIAS

In Damascus there was a disciple named Ananias. The Lord called to him in a vision, "Ananias!" "Yes, Lord," he answered. The Lord told him, "Go to the house of Judas on Straight Street and ask for a man from Tarsus named Saul, for he is praying. In a vision he has seen a man named Ananias come and place his hands on him to restore his sight." "Lord," Ananias answered, "I have heard many reports about this man and all the harm he has done to your saints in Jerusalem. And he has come here with authority from the chief priests to arrest all who call on your name." But the Lord said to Ananias, "Go! This man will be my chosen instrument to carry my name before the Gentiles and their kings and before the people of Israel. I will show

him how much he must suffer for my
name."
—Acts 9:10–16

Who are the little people in the Bible that we often forget?

The most famous conversion experience was the
murderous Saul becoming the apostle Paul. But it all
happened because of Ananias. The light did not change
Saul to Paul. It would be the work of a man named
Ananias who would be called to *get up and go* place his
hands on Saul and heal him. Ananias would be the hands
and feet and voice of God inviting Saul to change his
ways. Don't you know Ananias quaked in his sandals at
his call to touch the villain? He saw the vision and was
willing to face his fears. God used him in a mighty way.
What a call!

It makes us wonder how we would have responded.

- What if God called you into mission to serve
  people who hated the Christian faith? What
  would you say to God?
- What if Ananias did not get up and go? We would
  not have half the New Testament written by this
  blind man named Saul.

PRAYER

Thank you for Ananias, God. He was a huge part of the
greatest story of transformation. If you can use him, can

you use me? Who is someone who despises the Christian faith? What if I was the one who was called to go to that person and help clear that one's blindness? Or who has come my way to clear my blind spots? Hear my prayer, God …

HOLY SPIRIT SHAKEDOWN

> Then Ananias went to the house and entered it. Placing his hands on Saul, he said, "Brother Saul, the Lord—Jesus, who appeared to you on the road as you were coming here—has sent me so that you may see again and be filled with the Holy Spirit."
>
> —Acts 9:17

We can imagine Ananias having to get his courage up to enter the guest home of the archenemy of the Christian movement. Did he want to turn around? Of course he did. Did he fear for his life? Surely he had doubts that what he had heard was his call. But he went. He placed his shaking hands on Saul. What did Saul look like? Was he not weak from fasting? Was Saul in a corner shivering in fear from the blinding light or personal words from Jesus himself? Was he repeating what he had heard? "Why are you persecuting me?"

When Ananias touched Saul, he made his mission clear. He was not there for any other reason than to follow God's commands. And those commands were to help Saul to see and to be filled with the Holy Spirit. God had every right to send Ananias to that home to kill Saul and string him up for killing Stephen and other Christians. But God did not. God showed his power by changing Saul into Paul, the great missionary of the early church. Put your hand on the wall of that home, and feel the Holy Spirit shakedown!

- Have you ever been asked to go into a tough situation and face your fears?
- Has God led you to speak the truth in a hostile environment?
- Have you been like Ananias and sensed a need to go where no one else has gone before?
- If so, then you have been a part of the Holy Spirit shakedown, where God is moving to restore broken people to wholeness.

Well done! Keep it up!

PRAYER

God, this scene with Ananias and Saul needs to be remembered. You used Ananias as your instrument so you could use Saul as your instrument. Both of them were keys to the progression of the Gospel to the Gentiles. Thank you for this story. And thank you for letting them open the door to me too ...

GET THE BAGPIPER

> Immediately, something like scales
> fell from Saul's eyes, and he could see
> again. He got up and was baptized, and
> after taking some food, he regained his
> strength.
> —Acts 9:18–19

While he was blind, he could not get up. He was down
and out. He was wounded, humiliated, and unable to eat
or drink anything. He had lost for the first time in his
adult life. The champion of the faith, the captain of the
religious sect, was knocked for a loop. But as soon as he
could see, he sprang to his feet, jumped into the baptismal
font, ate a lunch, and was on his way! He could see. He
could swim. He could feast!

When God changes a person, sometimes it is immediate.

If we want to make a change, we can do it cold turkey
sometimes. If we want to quit a bad habit, sometimes we
can never return. God can drop the scales off our eyes,

and we can see life as God would see life. When we get myopic, God opens us to see more and to see again immediately.

Have you experienced a time when the light went on and you saw again with new vision? Is there a bad habit you would like to quit? Why do we return to our old ways when God is waiting to make us healthy? Let's remember Saul and how immediately he could see life again. Do you wonder what he said to Ananias, who led him to Christ?

Get the bagpiper! It's time to hear the famous melody. Let's retell the story of Saul today and sing out loud the hymn of "Amazing Grace": "I was blind, but now I see!"

Is that your story? Can you relate? Have you seen the light and been opened to God all around you, living in the ones you despised? Have you shared your story with anyone lately?

PRAYER

God, what a miracle! You took a mean killing machine of a man and humbled him so he could be restored for you. He would go on and change the world in your name! Thank you for reminding us that everyone we meet is redeemable!

LOOK FOR THE OPENING

After many days had gone by, the Jews conspired to kill him, but Saul learned of their plan. Day and night they kept close watch on the city gates in order to kill him. But his followers took him by night and lowered him in a basket through an opening in the wall.

—Acts 9:23–25

Saul was learning what it meant to be a disciple of Jesus. He would be persecuted. As Jesus said, "You will be my witness." Saul discovered he would be willing to die for the testimony of what Jesus was doing in his life. The predator had become the prey. They smelled blood in the water, and the sharks were circling. They stood by the gates waiting for their chance.

Maybe you feel that way. You are making a turn toward God, but there are folks around you who want to kill your spirit. How do you escape from the ones who are out to get you?

Saul had new friends in the faith who would help him live! They would lower him in a basket. Picture that. How many did it take to hold that line above him? What trust it took for Saul to get in that basket and believe they would not throw him off the side.

The phrase that sticks out is "through an opening in the wall." God provided an opening. And where was that opening? In the wall, which seemed so closed. It was the hole in the wall that Saul found to escape his death. When it seems like all is closed and there is no hope, look for an opening in the wall. Saul was opened in more ways than one.

- Is there a story in your life in which you discovered an escape route from old living to new living?
- Would you like to share that story with God or with a friend?

PRAYER

God, where is the opening for me? Help me to not be so closed. Thank you also for people who are helping me live fully.

MISSION WINS

As the Father has sent me, I am
sending you.
—John 20:21

We have walked with Jesus and the early church to
discover that mission wins. Anytime we expand our
horizons and listen to that small voice of God nudging
us outward, we meet fascinating people and see where
God is at work.

Reading scripture through the filter of mission is a good
way to love God and our neighbors and to get away from
thinking only of ourselves. When God calls us into full-
time ministry (that is everybody), he calls us into seeing
our mission at home, on the job, at the ball fields, with
the bridge clubs, and at the dance recitals. Wherever we
go, God is sending us!

In each of these devotionals, the common theme is clear:
God calls us to get up and go with him into the great
unknown on the road in between faith and life. You

have been comforted and challenged in these stories and invited to see yourself in the dramas that unfold.

God is ahead of us. He leads us by going in front while looking back to see if we are still following. Are you close to Jesus, or is there a distance? Are you trying to go ahead of God in your life, making all the moves, deciding for yourself without asking God for direction?

I hope these devotionals and prayers have enabled you to engage in the mission between the Gospel and culture. If you have been touched by these messages, then look around in your community at places where God is already blessing, and volunteer. Join a Relay for Life team; serve in a soup kitchen or a shelter. Sign up to be a big sister or a big brother in a local neighborhood. Teach at a dyslexia clinic, or go on a mission trip. Come cheer on those in the Special Olympics. These are just a few mission moments to keep us out of the rut and onto the road of inspiration and hope.

BENEDICTION

You go nowhere by accident.
Wherever you go, God is sending you.
God has a purpose in your being there.
And he has given his Holy Spirit to you!

GET UP AND
GO WITH US

Here are some resources for your journey to go deeper into mission:

Missional Church Information (These are just a few great resources available.)
Missional Church Article by Tim Keller (Trianglecpn.org)
Missional Church Network
(MissionalChurchNetwork.com)
Missional Church by Darrell L. Guder

Media
PavingYourWay.com offers sixty-second *Hush in the Rush* moments and a thirty-minute *Road in Between* show sharing mission stories of Christ's love and encouragement.

Mission Trips
Rivers of the World (ROW.org) offers trips around the world blending medicine, education, construction and ministry.

Reaching Our World's Kids (ROWKids.org) offers trips to Central America emphasizing education, clean water projects, medicine, and construction.

Church Ministry
The Christian Church (Disciples of Christ) (Disciples.org)

Books by Tom Sikes (Available on Amazon.com and iUniverse.com.)
Hush in the Rush: 52 Quiet Times for Busy People
Wind Chimes
Welcome Home: Meditations Along Your Way

Contact Us: PavingYourWay.com
Facebook: Paving Your Way, Road in Between and Hush in the Rush

Made in the USA
Lexington, KY
28 September 2015